LIFE WITHOUT FEAR

by Mike Dalton and Mickey Fowler

LIFE
WITHOUT
FEAR

by
Mike Dalton and Mickey Fowler

ISI PUBLICATIONS
P.O. BOX 5254, MISSION HILLS, CALIFORNIA 91345
A Division of
INTERNATIONAL SHOOTISTS INC.

Photos by Ichiro Nagata
Outlined with Roger Keiper

LIFE WITHOUT FEAR

First Printing, April 1983
Second Printing, September 1983
Third Printing, November 1984
Copyright ©1983 ISI Publications
Mission Hills, CA 91345

ISBN 0-9610954-0-7

LIBRARY OF CONGRESS CATALOG CARD NUMBER 83-80780

PRINTED IN THE UNITED STATES OF AMERICA

ACKNOWLEDGMENTS

We wish to express our sincere appreciation to our wives and families for their unwavering support during the completion of this book. We are indeed fortunate to be blessed with such exceptional individuals.

We, also, gratefully acknowledge the efforts of many of our friends for their contributions toward this work. Especially Ichiro Nagata, photography and William R. Ramsey, attorney at law.

Mickey Fowler   Mike Dalton

ABOUT THE AUTHORS

Mickey Fowler, a three time **Bianchi Cup Champion,** holder of the prestigious **Combat Master** ranking, all time top money winner in practical pistol competition, 1979 U.S. National Combat Shooting Champion, 1983 World Speed Shooting Champion (Steel Challenge), is recognized as the top professional pistol shooter in the world today.

Mike Dalton has been one of the most consistent top competition shooters in the world for many years. He is a four time **Southwest Pistol League Champion,** holds the prestigious rank of **Combat Master,** is a two time member of the U.S. World Combat Shooting Team, and holds numerous national and international records.

Both have won the much coveted **Colt Firearms Speed Shooting Championship** at the Bianchi Cup International Pistol Tournament. Mickey won it in 1982 and Mike in 1983.

They also operate the internationally renowned International Shootists, Inc., training school, which has produced more world class shooters than any other training facility. Their training courses have attracted students from all over the world. Their intent is to provide responsible citizens with the best possible handgun training available.

The National Rifle Association has certified them as N.R.A. Rifle, Pistol and Shotgun Instructors, thus showing their expertise with all types of firearms.

Their winning techniques have brought them more tournament wins than any other training organization's staff. This is what really sets ISI apart from other training facilities. All staff instructors are current pistol champions of combat shooting.

Over the years, many students from all over the world and all walks of life have attended their classes and have learned the necessary skills to defend themselves with a handgun. This book is a result of the experience they have gained as pistol champions and from passing their skills on to others. While there are other instructors of combat shooting, only those who have explored the outer limits of the handgun's capability can understand the vast expanse of the subject.

The shooting techniques used by Mike and Mickey have proven their worth in open competition on numerous occasions. Many of these skills are directly parallel to self defense shooting.

The International Shootists Inc. Cannon Safe Co. four man pistol team led by Mickey and Mike are current World Champions and have won more championships than any other team in the history of practical shooting. Their methods clearly work in these "test conditions" of world class competition and are not unproven theory.

Mike is the "Gun Editor" for **Gun Owner Magazine** and Mickey is a regular columnist for **American Handgunner Magazine.** Both are contributing authors to various national and international publications.

FOREWORD

The purpose of this book is to provide you with the knowledge you will need to effectively use the handgun for self defense. We do not expect to avoid criticism when dealing with a subject of such importance. There will be those who will claim we advocate killing and compare us to extremist groups. Those in favor of gun confiscation as a supposed crime deterrent will accuse us of promoting counter productive anti-crime measures. Nothing could be farther from the truth!

In October of 1982, the Rand Corporation released a six year study of crime. This was conducted and paid for by the United States Government. The results both bear out the need for effective self defense, and contradict the pro-gun control groups' claim that by severely restricting the number of handguns, crime can be reduced. Basically, the report stated that the only way to decrease crime is to put those who commit violent crimes, or are repeat felons in prison with stricter sentencing. It was also stated that the majority of crimes were done by a minority of professional hard-core criminals. The report did not show any reduction in violent crimes in cities with populations over 500,000 which had strict gun control laws. Some of these cities such as New York, Boston, and Washington, D.C. have openly admitted to the complete failure of gun control as a crime deterrent. Gun control advocates, however, always seem to produce statistics in their campaigns which contradict independent studies, and are biased, prejudicial, and unverifiable.

On the other extreme, in Kennasaw, Georgia, a law was instituted in 1981, which required every adult to have a gun. This created an uproar among the gun control groups which included such irresponsible predictions as the residents of Kennasaw would not only be sorry, but many of them would die because of the presence of guns. The facts are in the first year of the law, violent crime and burglaries dropped 86%. There were no deaths caused by the mere presence of guns, and criminals certainly paid attention to the anti-criminal sentiment among the residents of Kennasaw. Granted, this is a small community, but a Federal Criminal Justice report stated that cities with stringent gun control laws have a higher rate of violent crime. Obviously these statistics and independent reports show "gun control" does not deter criminal activity, and claims that it does should be deleted from bigoted gun control campaigns.

Common sense tells us gun control is politically more favorable in that it doesn't raise taxes as much as building the much needed prisons would. It's simple, we have to fight violent criminals in effective ways, not with shortsighted rhetoric. As a rule, most of the people who want to take away your right to own a handgun know nothing about guns. This is clearly demonstrated by the statements they make. One example we are told is instead of using a handgun for self defense, we should use a rifle or shotgun. Anyone knowledgeable will tell you although a long gun is much more deadly, it is also more dangerous to use for self defense. The recoil on a long gun is much more intense, and too much to handle for many people, especially the elderly or handicapped. Also, a bullet from a rifle can travel through several walls injuring people in another room, even another home. But we are told that the handgun's ease of concealability is why it must be banned.

The truth is, the only difference between the concealability of a long gun and a hand gun is a hacksaw. They also tell us the chances are if a gun is kept for self defense, the citizen is more likely to injure himself than an intruder. We will concede that some people are not responsible enough to properly and safely use a gun, and we are sure the gun control advocates will concede this holds true in other areas such as driving, child raising, and so on. The statistics they quote fail also to recognize an important fact. Most times the mere presence of a gun in the hands of a responsible citizen has saved lives. It has prevented a potentially violent situation from escalating and getting out of control. In other words, most self defense situations involving a gun do not result in a shooting, but end without shots being fired. This is conveniently forgotten by our anti-gun elitists.

It is a sad commentary on America that our criminal justice system is such a failure, and so many of us are justified in feeling compelled to buy guns for self defense. It is also a disappointment there are so few areas in this country where you can feel absolutely safe. You do, of course, have the right to be defenseless and throw yourself upon the mercy of a violent criminal. You have the right to give up your self respect and beg to be spared. You may only be rewarded with a beating or you and your loved ones may be killed. You have that right, but some of us don't want to be sheep being led to slaughter. People who take away your right to own a handgun are in effect saying that self defense is not a right but a privilege. It is very easy for politicians to tell you this while surrounded by armed bodyguards. The right to survival has been one of the most basic rights of man since first entering the world.

If anyone believes that violent crime won't ever touch his life, he only has to read the paper or listen to the news for proof that anyone can be a victim. If he still doesn't believe it, he is either a fool or a complete idiot. If someone is naive enough to think he can fend off a violent attacker with words while waiting for the police to arrive, he just doesn't comprehend the real world. The police are brave individuals who do the best job possible, but they are under paid and overworked. They can't be everywhere at once, and as a result rarely respond soon enough to stop a violent criminal.

No one has the right to take away the honest citizen's guns even if he wishes to replace them with some other means of self defense. It is your right to choose what method you feel is best for your personal defense. Making self defense a political ball game, and trying to take away one of our basic rights is a crime.

By possessing the knowledge needed to use a handgun for self defense, you don't have to rely on the whim of some psychotic killer as to whether or not you will survive. You will now have the means to control the situation and ensure the survival of yourself and your loved ones. We are not advocating you go looking for trouble, but neither do you have to crawl if trouble finds you. We do advocate the use of a handgun for self defense in a last resort situation, and we strongly believe that you have the right to defend your life.

For many of you, the terminology contained in this book will be new. A complete glossary of terms in the back has been provided to help eliminate any confusion you might have. Also, we have recommended a variety of equipment throughout this book, and the names and addresses of those mentioned along with a list of reputable gunsmiths will appear in the Resource Guide.

As you will soon notice, when referring to an assailant, we use the pronoun "he," rather than the cumbersome "he or she." We do not want to create the misconception that only men are criminals, or that most criminals are men; women can be just as dangerous. Because there is no neuter pronoun, we have used "he" where necessary.

This book was written for the novice as well as the more experienced shooter. The techniques and styles described are the most up to date and have proven to be superior methods of firing the handgun fast and accurately. The tactics are designed specifically for you, the private citizen whose only intention is surviving a lethal confrontation. By following and practicing the guidelines provided, you can become with practice, a good marksman, and possess knowledge which will help you survive a lethal attack. For the women, we have a special chapter devoted to their particular needs concerning self defense which has been widely praised by women from all walks of life. We are confident you will not only learn the desired shooting skills you need for self defense, but also learn a new awareness of the world which surrounds all of us.

TABLE OF CONTENTS

An armed criminal making forced entry into a potential victim's home. What would you do in a similar situation? With proper training you can greatly improve your ability to survive such a situation.

CHAPTER 1

NO OTHER CHOICE

Violent crime is not going away and unfortunately it could do away with you. An assailant can and will selfishly decide when, where, and whom to attack as well as the method to be used. The potential victim's method of self defense is too often guided by morals and ethics not shared by the assailant. The untrained private citizen finds it easy to sit back when discussing the possibility of a life and death situation and boast that he would not hesitate to defend himself in whatever manner was necessary. Many even boast that they would kill without hesitation if necessary and never give it a second thought. All this is a pipedream and a very dangerous one at that. The gun wielding private citizen is no safer against an armed assailant than one who is confronted and cornered stark naked unless he:

1. Knows how to use his weapon
2. Has the proper understanding of a combat situation
3. Has preplanned the proper course of action
4. Has a thorough understanding of the meaning of survival.

How to use a handgun is detailed throughout this book. Even though we listed it as number one, we feel number two, **the proper understanding of a combat situation,** will give you the incentive to thoroughly read and reread, as necessary, every word in this book until you are sure you have this understanding.

Survival is not a subjective grey area to be discussed in an intellectual arena with morals, religious beliefs, and psychological theories intertwined. It might make for good cocktail party conversation but that never saved anyone's life. Survival is a simple, cold fact. You either want to survive, believe you have the right to survive, or, in a life and death situation, you will likely die.

There are approximately five million individuals out there, enjoying freedom at your expense, who carry illegal weapons. For every one of

1

them there is another who can get an illegal weapon anytime he wants. There are many more who are just as dangerous without a gun as with one. None of these individuals is affected by gun control. These people are your enemy, they are lawbreakers, and the current laws do not restrain them. Instead, they almost encourage them. Until our legislators turn their anti-crime rhetoric into prisons to house and separate violent criminals from society and the judicial system keeps them there as long as necessary, you could be their victim.

You have to understand everything about the enemy. Walking free in our society are individuals who place no value on human life, not even their own. Your life means nothing to them. You are prey for them to feed on. This is a fact that is hard for the average citizen to understand. We go through life socializing with individuals who are basically decent, like ourselves. But, there are individuals who don't have the same values. You only have to read the newspaper or watch television to see only a fragment of the hideous crimes which take place around you every day. You say it won't happen to you, but it happens to people just like yourself. One day, it could be you.

In the last decade, violent crime has risen drastically. You very well might know someone who has been a victim, if not, more than likely, a violent crime has occurred to someone at sometime in the area where you live. Whether it's rape, murder, aggravated assault, or a variety of other undesirable choices, you must be aware that it could be you as part of your preparation for self defense. The desire to survive must be absolute. Self defense is mostly a state of mind; awareness and the determination to survive are vitally important. You must be able to make the moral judgment that it is your right to survive. No one has the right to take your life without possible peril to his own. If someone chooses to violently attack you, you must be able to survive.

To survive you would greatly benefit from us telling you how to identify the enemy. We wish we could. You can usually pick out the "bad guys" on television or in the movies. This is not the case in the real world. You might feel that you are good at first impression. Are you sure enough to bet your life on it? We hope not! The point is simple, you are not a professional when it comes to law enforcement. The truth is the police are trained to trust no one, and their life depends on this rule. The best dressed, most articulate, harmless looking person could be dangerous. No one is a professional when it comes to identifying a criminal until a crime is in progress and then, for the victim, it is too late. The criminal, however, is a professional and in business to rob, rape, or murder. He is not going to be visible in such a way as to allow a potential victim of a crime to identify his intentions until it is too late. Even the few criminals who are easily identifiable will hide their intentions. Particularly in urban areas, if you avoided every person who looked to be down on his luck, you'd have no place you could walk comfortably! There is no stereotype. There is nothing we can tell you other than to trust no stranger at anytime. If adults followed the same instructions they give to their children about strangers, there would be fewer rapes and violent crimes simply because they would not be as accessible as they often make themselves now.

Obviously there is no way to avoid a determined criminal. If you are confronted, what can you expect? Expect the worst from any person who is acting in a dangerous manner. There are as many different types of criminals as there are crimes they commit. First, and most dangerous, is the **hardened criminal.** These are generally repeat offenders who have spent plenty of time in jail. **You are spit to them.** They have probably spent years in jail, planning criminal activities, and upon their release are intent on doing whatever is necessary to avoid going back. This includes the killing of any and all witnesses, regardless of necessity. Recently, a convicted murderer admitted to killing a blind man he knew was blind because he feared the blind man would identify his voice.

A second type, usually found in urban areas, are **gangs.** We all read about this alarming problem. Killing is part of their membership requirements. If you live in a nice suburban area, don't feel like this doesn't affect you. More and more these gangs are going into what is known as high stake areas. These areas include your nice, comfortable neighborhood. The term "high stakes" refers to the fact that they run a higher risk of getting caught in these areas. They have taken into consideration this factor along with the fact that these areas are more profitable to rob. The profit they stand to gain takes precedence and the higher chance of getting caught makes it a more prestigious act in their eyes. Robbery, rape and murder are a deadly game to them and you are the toy they play with. Social workers give a lot of fancy explanations for this type of phenomenon. They constantly refer to socio-economic factors combined with a variety of cultural influences. That's fine and dandy, and it may be true, but if it's your life or theirs, don't hesitate and become a statistic they use in one of their philosophical arguments.

In addition to hardened criminals and gangs, we have the criminal involved in drug related crimes. These people come in two shades of death black. One is an **addict** who commits crimes to support his habit. Plain and simple, he is desperate, selfish, and insane with the delirium caused by his drug induced needs. He or she might point a gun at you and fall crying to the ground, begging for mercy, or maybe they will pull the trigger or attack you with whatever means available. The other is the **drug user** who can be either an addict or an occasional user. Both are equally dangerous, particularly those under the influence of hallucinogenic drugs such as PCP, now in rampant use. These people can be absolute maniacs without any weapon other than their bare hands. They have been known to break handcuffs and continue to fight while bleeding to death from multiple gun shot wounds. They have super-human strength and a dehumanized, barbaric attitude. No matter how harmless they might act, under no condition can they be trusted; they can transform instantly into an enraged killer.

We conducted an interview with an urban police officer about the behavior and attitudes among criminals he had come into contact with during his twenty years on the police force.

Q: What is your view about the hardened criminal and what might the average person expect if faced by one of these individuals?

A: I think that they can be very unpredictable. When I say unpredictable I'm talking about no matter what they do or say, they might act in the opposite manner.

Q: Is this because they don't plan what they are going to do?

A: No, not at all, they act in a very calculated manner. They try to get an arresting officer or a potential victim off guard. The hardened criminals have already gone through the system and basically know what they can get away with and what they can't get away with and, therefore, are more likely to commit a violent crime in comparison, to say, the occasional burglar.

Q: Do you think that the majority of burglaries of homes are committed by hardened criminals?

A: Well, statistics show that actually the greatest number of burglaries in the home and crimes of this sort are committed by juveniles.

Q: Are juveniles, despite their ages, to be considered, for the most part, hardened criminals?

A: That really is impossible to answer. In certain areas, ones you would call slums, many are hardened criminals, but you also have juveniles who really have no idea of right or wrong for some unknown reason. These juveniles might not have the tendency to be violent or may actually be more frightened by surprising someone in a home they illegally entered than is the innocent party. But, then again, you have juveniles who think it's all a big game and wouldn't hesitate to harm an innocent party. Juveniles, as a general rule, aren't as specific about the items they will take as are the hardened criminals. Most hardened criminals will specialize in particular items where he has a fence waiting to purchase them. They prefer to steal items which are not identifiable, such as jewelry and cash. A good example is what we call a hot prowl burglar. He usually takes money. He won't take credit cards or anything else, just cash.

Q: Can these Hot Prowlers be dangerous?

A: If you corner them, definitely. The Hot Prowler isn't what I would call violent as a rule, in that he won't hunt down someone in the house.

Q: So, if a homeowner heard an intruder in the house you would suggest that he doesn't try to hunt down the intruder?

A: No, under no circumstances. The best thing would be to call the police. That's our job.

Q: What is your feeling about a responsible adult purchasing a handgun for self defense?

A: An adult, well, there is nothing wrong with learning how to use a handgun for self defense or personal enjoyment. If you are going to acquire a firearm, I think it is extremely important that you not only learn how to use it, but that you try to make yourself mentally prepared. You need to know how to shoot and shoot well. Someone should not go out and buy a handgun with the idea that once I bring it home and someone breaks in they've had it. Without practice and training as well as psychological preparation, statistics show that, an individual who is not prepared to use a firearm in self defense is likely to fail at his objective.

Q: Have you been involved in any shooting incidents yourself?

A: Just one.

Q. What goes on in your mind as it all takes place?

A: In my case, we had some time to think. The suspect was armed with a knife and very distraught. We had several opportunities that would have given us cause to shoot him but we didn't. We continually ordered him to drop the weapon, but he was totally out of his head and refused. Eventually he came at me. I backed off and backed off. I didn't want to shoot him, no police officer wants to shoot anyone. We aren't the blood thirsty killers like a lot of people think. Anyway, he backed off at one point, and I guess he decided he was going to end it all, and he was going to use the police to execute him. This happens a lot, anyway, he made the statement, "let's get it over with," and then he proceeded to charge at me and the other officers. We had no choice but to defend ourselves using deadly force. Most shootings occur in a split second. You really don't have time to think other than during the circumstances leading up to a shooting. You walk up to a car and suddenly a guy pulls a gun, and before you know it your gun is in your hand. It's either him or you and that's it.

Q: So you have an instinctive reaction based on your experience and training?

A: That's exactly right. You usually, in most cases, have no time to think, you only have time to react.

Q: If a citizen is armed and in his home and he is aware an intruder is in the house, what should he tell the police when he calls them?

A: He should give the police officer on the phone a description of himself, what he is wearing, that he is armed, that way one of the officers who respond to his call for assistance knows that he is armed and what he looks like. When the police arrive, the best and most important thing for him to do would be, put the weapon away. Set it down, put it in his waistband, anything but continue to have it in his hand. Also, when approaching an officer, have your hands visible. Most people, unfortunately, see the police have arrived and go running outside with their hands waving, extremely excited; too often they never put the gun away and are unknowingly waving the gun around. This can cause real problems for everyone. The best thing to do is put the gun away, walk slowly to the police, tell them you are the one who called and that you are armed.

Q: Let's say that a citizen has a gun and has captured an intruder. What should he do?

A: Well, if the criminal decided he is going to give it up and wait until the police arrive, the citizen should stay away from him, because the closer you get to him the more likely the criminal is going to change his mind and attempt to get the gun away from you. The closer you get, the more opportunity the criminal has of successfully disarming you, and obviously if you stay away from him he would be less likely to have the opportunity to get the gun and, as a result, less likely to try anything. If he should try to get away, don't shoot him. As long as he is not acting in an aggressive manner towards you, don't shoot him because you will be the one who suffers in the long run. The best thing is stay far away so that he can't rush or lunge at you.

Q: Do you find that some people are more preoccupied with trying to capture a criminal than with their own safety at times?

A: Yes, I think some people get so excited that they are going to catch this bad guy that they don't think enough about what they are doing and, as a result, don't protect themselves. They don't stop to think that they are dealing with not only a dangerous individual but also a desperate one. It's the same as cornering a wild animal. Then if they do capture them, they sometimes let their guard down, which is something you never can do. Other times they run after this guy, capture him out on the street somewhere, and then find themselves wondering what to do next. You don't have any handcuffs, you don't have a telephone or any line of communication. What you have is a real problem. An uncuffed, dangerous individual and nothing but time on your hands until someone notices you. Another obvious problem is if a citizen or police officer spots you holding a gun on someone else, you look like the assailant. It just isn't a good idea at all.

Q. A lot of police departments are involved in neighborhood watch programs. Have you found them to be effective?

A: I think the program is very good. They do the best they can to train these citizens how to observe. The best thing these citizens can do is become the eyes and ears of the police department because we can't be everywhere at once. The police department tries to get as many citizens involved as possible. They tell them how to protect themselves and if they just follow the prescribed simple steps it is a big aid to the department and the neighborhood in general. You can't fully protect your home against a possible break in, but you can make it as difficult as possible. In having to break a lock or window, dodge a barking dog, you increase the chance that a fellow neighbor will see this and phone the police when you have a neighborhood watch program.

Q: I'm sure that you have had contact with criminals who have committed serious crimes who are either back out on the street after serving their sentences or are now serving time.

A: Yes, quite a bit.

Q: Do they ever express any remorse about what they have done?

A: Not the hardened criminal who has been through the system several times. I don't think they have any consciences. I don't think any rehabilitation program is going to change them. The first time offender who finally gets caught and does some time, will once in awhile show some remorse and maybe will respond to an attempt at rehabilitation. If they don't, from there on out it becomes less likely they will. The hardened criminal simply doesn't care and doesn't know or want any other way of life other than crime.

Q: What about drugs and the behavior patterns concerning those engaged in a criminal activity while under the influence?

A: Well, those under the influence of PCP, for example, are completely out of it. They don't know what they're doing, they are completely out of it. Other drugs, such as barbiturates, which are depressants, have a tendency to simply slow down, although after continual use it really doesn't depress their systems. Different types of drugs cause different behavior. You never really know what to expect and in spite of what someone might tell you that he's on, many times they don't even remember what they took.

Q: What about security companies. Are they all pretty good or only some?

A: I think the patrol security companies, those being private patrols that check doors and answer calls, are only as good as the men they hire. I have found that most security guards that are hired to, let's say, work at gates, department stores, etc., have little or no training and very few have any experience in the field of security and are not even good observers. I find that many times a private citizen will be more helpful as far as observing a crime that took place than the security guard who was hired to do just that. A lot of them are old men or aspiring dropouts from the police academy. Too often they are disgruntled people who wanted to be policemen but didn't have the necessary qualifications. Most companies don't pay these people very much and as a result don't attract better qualified people. The more sophisticated security systems who provide better training and pay more get better people.

Q: If an adult decided to arm himself for self defense, what would you suggest?

A: I think they would be much better off with a handgun. It is a much more effective method of stopping an attack than mace or other such methods. It's more comfortable and if you get proficient with it, it is just as good as a shotgun or a rifle. A shotgun spreads too much and a rifle produces too much velocity and creates a danger from the standpoint of distance it can travel whether it goes through an obstruction or not.

Q: If you had only one thing to say was the most important as far as surviving and protecting yourself against an attack, what would it be?

A: I think the most important thing is common sense. If you use common sense you won't have problems, and if you do, it will be much less likely to be a serious problem. More people get into serious trouble because they fail to realize their own limitations. You have to know what you are capable of. You can take stock by envisioning how you would react to a situation. It really falls into the category of preplanning, something which is stressed in all police training. Knowledge and experience are great assets, but the average citizen doesn't have a working knowledge or experience with criminals.

Q: Everyone knows that the crime rate is constantly rising, far in excess of the proportionate increase in the population. Why do you think this is?

A: It really is the court system. Police officers often feel like they are just throwing sand from one end of the beach to the other. We arrest someone and they get off on a technicality. We arrest someone for armed robbery, they are convicted but are released on parole in six months and are back in business. It's a light slap on the wrist for the criminal and they are back out on the street through the revolving door of our court system. I'll give you an example. Let's say someone is arrested for an outstanding warrant on a moving violation. If his car is impounded it can't be searched for drugs unless we can prove we have probable cause, a reason to believe there are drugs in this person's car. If the individual is searched, as all suspects must be upon arrest, and you feel a vial in a pocket, you know these vials are used to carry cocaine, amphetamines, even heroin, you can't arrest the individual for that. You can't ask him to take it out until he is actually booked. Once you take the individual to the station on a traffic violation he has a certain amount of time to produce bail before he can be booked and you can search him. If he produces bail during this time, usually about two hours, he walks out with the illegal substance, as they usually do. If a man committed an armed robbery and gets rid of the gun before he is caught, he probably will not be convicted of armed robbery. The technicalities are another area such as reading someone their rights. Sometimes if an officer, after a very dangerous capture, fails to immediately do this, the accused will find he's off scot free regardless of the number of witnesses. I can understand not allowing a statement made to a police officer who failed to read someone his rights, but it is beyond me to understand how all the other evidence and all the witnesses testimony can be discounted. The biggest problem is that if a criminal is convicted, he just doesn't spend enough time in jail if any time at all.

Q: Let's say I'm an upper middle class person who, for whatever reason, decides that crime pays. I don't have a record and I stick to unarmed burglaries. Where is the deterrent factor?

A: Unfortunately, there is virtually none. As a first time offender, you might do six months to a year or you might not do any time. I don't think the case example you're talking about is really typical of the main problem. The one that is so frustrating is that these felons are continually going through the system year after year because of technicalities, parole, the early release program, etc. As I've said before, the first time offender, many times, will learn a lesson once he realizes he can get caught. Maybe he will learn a lesson, but how much of a lesson is serving a minimal sentence when you get caught for one crime knowing that you probably have committed quite a few before you did get caught? The others, who have been constantly in and out of jail, haven't learned anything except how to use the system. This is why you look at the present judicial system and wonder just what is going on.

Q: What do you think of the parole system?

A: For the purpose of rehabilitation, it's a joke. Twenty years ago, if you were convicted of burglary, you would probably spend at least five years in jail. Now your sentence by comparison is minimal and the same is true all the way up to murder. A prime example is the Onion Field murder of a police officer where one of the guys was paroled after serving twelve years. He murdered a policeman in cold blood! Simply, the parole system isn't working and our present sentencing structure isn't a deterrent to criminals.

Q: Do you think judges are too lenient?

A: Yes, definitely, and please print that. Too often it seems they take sides, almost always a side sympathetic towards a convicted criminal and the sentences are too lenient. Judges are supposed to be objective, to protect the accused's rights and to protect the citizens. I want the system to work, all police officers do. The judges have to get tough on convicted felons.

We all know that chances are we are in for real trouble when faced by a hardened criminal but, as you have just read, there is such an animal as the first time criminal. These types may not have the professional savvy or the hardened ruthlessness of the other group, but they can be just as dangerous. They can be the kind you may surprise by being home at the wrong time. The kind who might very well have no intention other than to rob your house. But how do you know whether or not he is dangerous or even for that matter an inexperienced criminal? YOU DON'T. Prepare for the worst, always prepare for the worst. You legally should give him the opportunity to run but if he doesn't, consider this. If someone has taken it upon himself to break into your home he is aware of the possibility of a confrontation, and he may be violent enough to kill. Your self defense tactics and the law section of this book will cover this area of how to proceed without needlessly endangering yourself.

The juvenile delinquent is not to be overlooked here. Although the laws are getting tougher, they aren't tough enough. Some juveniles are hardened criminals by puberty, others are robbing and raping for fun and profit. None of them wants to get caught! They might not be dangerous, but then again how many shootings have we heard about done at the hands of these young criminals? Enough for you to know they can be as much of a danger as an adult. Anyone can take a life regardless of his age. He is like any other person involved in criminal activities. You must prepare for the worst and utilize all self defense methods described in this book. What we are really saying is, in spite of the fact some criminals are more dangerous than others, your life depends on your ability to objectively evaluate anyone who comes in contact with you and react when justified. This attitude may seem cold, but it is the only realistic attitude. You will not have the time during a confrontation to discuss someone's motives. You have to prepare for the worst, you have to have no doubts about your right to survive. Only then will you be capable of doing so.

A serious problem women face is the threat of sexual assault. Many rapes are committed by acquaintances they think they know well enough to trust. Psychologists will tell you there are many mental disorders which are not easily detected. We aren't talking about the young man who delivers your groceries as much as we are talking about someone whom you might be about to date for the first time or someone you have been dating. We are also talking about casual acquaintances whom you may not date. We are not trying to breed a population of paranoid women; only to point out the need for awareness of this possibility. These men can be just as dangerous as anyone, maybe more so when their romantic intentions are rejected. There are many fine books available which discuss this subject in detail and provide some information on how to deal with this type of situation. We will confine our discussion of this to our method of self defense whether you are faced with the need for a deterrent or a more serious situation. Now that we have bombarded you with frightening information, let's take a look at the many methods available to protect and warn you, particularly when you are in your home. There are many security measures which can be taken but unfortunately they are never capable of saving your life. They are capable of providing a deterrent and giving you a warning. The security industry isn't going to like our appraisal, but it's about time someone put it in black and white. False alarms have become a tremendous problem. For the professional criminal they are no problem at all. The situation is simple. The more complicated they make these systems, the more that can go wrong, and the more false alarms. The high number of false alarms increase the workload of the police and they decrease the faith placed in the legitimacy of the alarm. The result is a response time that averages in the thirty to forty-five minute range. It has become such a problem that alarm owners are now fined in some areas for every false alarm over four a year. As for the criminal, who has adapted wonderfully, it actually became an advantage. They have been known to purposely set off these alarms, wait for the police to investigate and report it as a false alarm, then they go in and rob the house. Many cases have occurred in which they have set off these alarms so many times they have caused the alarm company, the police, and the homeowner to justifiably decide that the system is malfunctioning and turn it off. This has left the homeowner or the storekeeper totally unprotected until the service people get a chance to check it out.

Let's not overlook criminals who are capable of rewiring the security system. They do exist. While you sit inside your home, feeling impenetrable, your security system could actually be bypassed and your phone lines disconnected. This brings up another very big mistake many people make. Just because you have an expensive, supposedly "fool proof" system, you still have to take ordinary precautions of locking your doors. Every precaution you take could give you the time you need to prepare for the worst. In defense of security systems, we will admit that they can act as a deterrent and as a warning system and this is an important asset. More importantly, even though statistics show they reduce the likelihood of forced entry into your home, what happens if you are unlucky enough to be on the wrong side of the statistics? You might not survive long enough to even regret it. Dogs are an excellent alarm system, but only act as an alarm. Trained attack dogs can be dangerous and unpredictable. Even the best trained animals are still animals who act upon instinct. Aside from the individual the dog is trained to obey, he presents a serious threat of death and injury to another member of your family and anyone visiting your home. We advise a good house dog over a trained attack dog. Like attack dogs, they instinctively will establish territorial rights only those known to them will be able to enter, without their barking. But, they can't attack, is the argument we often hear. No, they usually aren't trained to do this and some dogs won't attack, but neither can an attack dog who is drugged, poisoned, or persuaded in a variety of ways to become preoccupied. One method which has been used on male attack dogs is to drop a female over the fence who is in heat. It works. The animal's instinct to enjoy a little recreational pleasure dominates his desire and training to perform his duties as a guard dog. A good dog as an alarm is probably a more reliable warning system than the most expensive security system. It is also a very visible deterrent to any intruder. This does and will make a difference.

Security gates and security windows are another booming industry. Yes, it will take a criminal more time to penetrate but it can cause several problems to you also. The biggest disadvantage is unless you use the more expensive fire excape security windows, where bars can be released from a lever on the inside of the window, there is an increased risk that you could be trapped in a room if there ever is a fire. The problem with the fire escape windows is how does a fire fighter get in? A problem with all security windows is there are many sophisticated cutting devices which can quickly take care of the bars. Security gates can be jumped and rewired to open. There is no fence made which a determined criminal can not jump over or cut through.

If you can afford a twenty-four hour a day armed body guard who you are sure can not be bribed, you might not need any other protection. San Francisco recently passed a ban-on-guns ordinance, and the Mayor made a big deal out of turning in her gun. The press did a great job reporting this. The reasoning they hoped to make others adopt was if the Mayor can feel safe enough to go about unprotected, shouldn't the average citizen? Yes, maybe the average citizen would feel just as safe as soon as they can afford armed body guards!

Neighborhood and Community Watch programs are well worth considering but, as a rule, they will not come under the realm of self defense. There are some areas in this country where a group of citizens have legally armed themselves and formed armed patrols for their neighborhoods. This can involve a great many legal problems and liabilities because these citizens may find themselves facing a wrongful death action. We are not saying that you should not go to the aid of a neighbor. We will cover this aspect thoroughly in our chapter on law.

Common place today are security buildings. Many have round the clock guards. But, as we have said, there are no security systems which are failsafe. Those with security guards may be somewhat safer than those without, but they are not failsafe. These systems have given many a false sense of security so that they become lax about locking their doors, are not as careful when parking their cars, don't check to see who is at their door before opening it, and feel they need no other protection.

We talked with the Regional Patrol Manager, Mike Fichman, of Westec Security in Los Angeles. His particular agency is considered one of the best in the country.

Q: What exactly does your security agency do?

A: We patrol the streets on a residential level only. We are somewhat like the old cops so to speak in that we have the time to check on things that the police no longer have the time to do. While they have calls stacked up on one another and one officer for several thousand citizens, we have an officer per every 3-5 hundred clients. Our officers go up and down the streets, investigating anything that does not look right at the homes of our clients. We have investigative rights on the property of clients, but on public streets or public property we have only the rights similar to a private citizen. We take calls that vary from vandalism and suspicious looking people to armed robbery in progress. As a rule, people know our response will be quicker than the police, being within one to six minutes after we are notified. Our clients are primarily upper middle class, and usually in the suburban areas. They pay a monthly service charge, approximately forty dollars per month for the top level of service, and they can call us every day twenty-four hours a day for any criminal activity or threat as well as a health emergency. What we really provide is two fold, first, a quick armed response to any type of criminal situation and, second, our mere presence in a neighborhood acts as a deterrent. By having a sign in front of their home announcing their security service, as well as the regular patrol of our officers in concentrated areas, it has proven to have made a difference.

Q: Is this service directly related to the installation of an electronic alarm system?

A: As a rule, yes, our company both sells and installs a large variety of systems. The patrol service can be purchased without the installation of an alarm system. Obviously, it is better to have an alarm system in coordination with the patrol and many people we service have both.

Q: How many officers do you have and what kind of training do they receive?

A: I have seventy-two officers under my supervision, all are trained in arms use and other aspects of law enforcement pertinent to residential security. This includes the use of handcuffs, baton, and we have a mandatory training course, which is very similar to most police academies. When I first came to the company, I came as the Range Master and helped set up the training program for new officers. I have also been involved in training private individuals concerning self defense with the handgun as well as training methods for the Southwest Pistol League and certain areas of law enforcement training methods. Personally, I have been shooting with the Southwest Pistol League for seven years and I hold the rank of Combat Master, of which only fifteen other people in the world also hold, and have set numerous records in major shooting competitions.

Q: That's quite an impressive background to draw on. What is your opinion on how good alarm systems are?

A: Some are excellent and others are virtually useless. In Southern California there are hundreds of alarm companies. Quite a few are fly by night operations, they start up and shut down just about that fast. There are only a handful that I would really term reputable. There are differences in equipment. One big advantage Westec has is that we design our own equipment. For instance, we have what we call talking alarms, designed so that while we are on the way to an alarm we can hear talking, screaming, etc., in the home itself. We have just about any type of security system you could want.

Q: What is the advantage of having a good electric alarm security system?

A: It puts up a line of first defense. Most criminals will go after the weakest opposition they can find. The very fact that you have a sign in front of your home of a reputable alarm company reduces the odds that you will be a victim. In having the exterior of your home alarmed, it gives you time to react on the inside as well as set into action a response from the police or the security company. Also, the audible sound of an alarm going off will scare away most intruders and alert the neighbors that there is a problem. There are also interior traps in a home, such as electronic beams placed in certain areas to protect against the possibility that someone has gained entrance by bypassing the exterior alarm without your knowledge.

Q: What about false alarms?

A: That's where you get into the problem of poorly made systems. Many of these new companies try to get by with poorly trained technicians and faulty equipment and this causes most of the problems. Los Angeles County, like many urban areas, now makes a homeowner take out a permit prior to the installation of an alarm system. They are fined after four false alarms in a twelve month period. Without the permit the police will no longer respond to an alarm. You can see an obvious advantage in choosing a security agency that responds to its own alarm system. We only call the police to respond to our alarms if we can not determine what the problem is or in the case of an actual arrest.

Q: Isn't it true that no matter how sophisticated a system may be there are some criminals who will go through it no matter what?

A: Well, yes, of course. Either they don't care or they think the police will take too long to respond. Those hyped up on drugs, who really aren't concerned about the consequences as much as they are about what they stand to gain, will.

Q: If someone has a highly sophisticated alarm system and a private armed patrol such as Westec, should they be concerned about self defense in their home?

A: Absolutely, I recommend that most of my clients learn how to use a handgun for self defense.

Q: That sounds contradictory to everything you've said.

A: It isn't at all. Even if a policeman or a security patrol is right in the neighborhood, the fastest response you are going to get is two or three minutes, and most crimes of violence will take place within two or three minutes. So, obviously, with all the protective measures taken, without taking it upon yourself to defend yourself, the violence could have already taken place and you are still a victim whether or not the individual is caught. It always comes down to the person in the home to realize that he is on his own until help arrives and because of this I recommend they arm themselves.

Q: What type of criminal element do you find in our supposedly safe suburban areas?

A: First of all, the old time cat burglars are a thing of the past. I'm talking about those who would never carry a gun, would never hurt anyone. The law itself has become such a revolving door situation that the penalties simply aren't acting as a deterrent to violent crime much less simple break and entry. Added to this fact is that there are criminals who will kill for kicks. There was recently a case where a homeowner had been shot, stabbed, well, you name it, and the assailant actually laughed and joked about it when apprehended. Too often we see criminals who have collected items in a home, have no reason to remain in the home, but upon hearing that someone is in the house, will hunt them down for no other purpose than to kill. The frightening thing about this is that this type of criminal could just as easily have left the home without confronting the hiding resident. There is a total ruthlessness out on the streets that didn't use to exist and isn't abating but increasing. They are very willing to sacrifice your life to gain possession of fifty dollars worth of items. They just do not fear the consequences of their act should they get caught.

Q: Have any of your officers become involved in a shooting?

A: We are very strict concerning our policies which will justify any

Westec patrolman drawing his weapon. As a rule, we do not condone the drawing of a weapon unless faced with deadly force. We are probably the strictest of any law agency, public or private and as a result we have had only two shooting incidents and no injuries sustained to any innocent parties. Both shooting incidents became necessary when the suspects were trying to use a firearm against us.

Q: I'm surprised you have had so few incidents. Why do you think your policies have been so successful?

A: Our people are taught to take control of any situation. With proper employment of law enforcement tactics, you really give a suspect no choice but to surrender peacefully, unless he's suicidal.

Q: Are there criminals who have adapted to sophisticated alarms and know how to bypass them undetected?

A: The sophisticated alarms, no. Again, the likelihood of this occurring depends on the soundness of the system as well as the company who installs it.

Q: Have you noticed that the criminal element from inner cities, such as gangs, are now leaving their areas and committing crimes in the suburbs?

A: Absolutely. In Los Angeles it's been nicknamed "the magic carpet ride." In other words, a home in Belair or Brentwood can be robbed, and the burglars can be home in their neighborhoods in ten to twenty minutes. Part of the growth of a suburban area is related to its development of highways in and out of the city. This also makes access for the criminal much easier prior to the time when they had lengthy drives in stop and go traffic. As a matter of fact, a highway in New York and New Jersey that would connect Newark to the suburbs was halted for that very reason. Another problem, unavoidable but still a problem, is the number of people which go in and out of the suburban areas. You have pool cleaners, gardeners, domestic help, and so on. This makes it difficult for neighbors to differentiate who belongs and who doesn't.

Q: The individuals you have apprehended, have you found they were often repeat offenders?

A: Definitely, over ninety percent have had prior convictions, many of them are armed and unlike the old time criminal I spoke of who would do everything they could to avoid a confrontation, many of today's criminals find the thought of an armed violent conflict exciting.

Q: What kind of weapons do they carry?

A: Primarily a cross between guns and knives, and we've seen every type of firearm used.

Q: Do they prefer handguns?

A: Yes, they are more concealable, so they have an obvious advantage.

Q: Won't gun control laws help control this problem?
A: Absolutely not. They will never have a problem getting a gun. What they don't steal they can easily obtain on the black market. It is so rampant that it just can't be stopped and even if it could someone with a moderate amount of gunsmithing knows how to make a gun out of scrap metal. It happens in prisons and it happens on the street. A case in point would be the "Zip" guns of the 50's.

Q: If I put in the most elaborate and sophisticated alarm system available, had a private patrol service, such as your company, and had a watch dog, why would I need to have a handgun for self defense?
A: As I have said, I recommend this to our clients. An alarm system, no matter how sophisticated, can only act as an alert, it can not physically prevent someone from gaining access to a home and committing an act of violence. Time is too short and life is too precious and vulnerable, in my opinion, to totally depend on a patrol service or the police to respond soon enough if the assailants keep on coming. When these things happen, they happen "right now" and you don't always have the luxury of waiting for help. When that moment comes, you better know how to defend yourself.

Q: What does the typical criminal look for when he's picking out a home to burglarize.
A: As a rule, they will avoid homes with a security system. It has been proven that if you take four homes, one of which doesn't have a security system, the one without a system is the most likely to be broken into. Criminals always pick the easiest or weakest victim. They also, as far as night burglars are concerned, avoid homes with good outside lighting. Obviously, if they are not on during the night hours they are of no use. Also, if they know the occupants are armed, they prefer to go to a home where they believe the occupants are unarmed.

Q: Do you find that criminals will pick out a particular neighborhood and rob it more than once as long as they are successful?
A: Definitely, groups of criminals from two to six in numbers who will pick out an area and literally feed on it for an extended period of time.

Q: How can they be so successful?
A: Well, they will pick out an area and then become very familiar with it. They will actually go up to homes in a variety of disguises, anything from a poll taker to a real estate agent claiming to have a buyer with a very high offer, and gain entrance to the home to case it and plan their robbery. People should always ask for identification and the best thing, really, is just not to let any stranger in your home unless it is a repair person or someone else you have requested. You'd be

surprised how many victims invite their attacker inside.

Q: Once a person has been robbed and the criminal successful in escaping do you think he will come back again?

A: From experience we have seen people who are robbed over and over again. It usually is because the house is seen as vulnerable because they have no dog, no alarm system, it may be secluded, have a poor lighting system, and any number of other factors that will serve to make it attractive to potential burglars.

Q: How do you choose your Westec officers?

A: We are very careful as far as their character and general background and their ability to perform in the field under stressful situations. At least fifty percent of our officers have a law enforcement background and all of our officers receive training at our own facility. We are the only agency I know of that does privately train its own people and it does make a difference.

Q: You have explained that your patrols work in selected areas and are very visible in those neighborhoods, has this effected attempted burglary rates in these areas?

A: Yes, in those neighborhoods we've gone into. The statistics bear out how the mere presence of signs in the yard and the high visibility of our cars patrolling concentrated areas have decreased crime in these areas noticeably. Some areas have gone from several burglaries a week to just two or three after a year since our service has entered the area.

Q: For those who can afford a security system and possibly a patrol service, what should they look for in a company?

A: They should look for an established company that has been around for awhile. You want to be sure about the equipment they use, can it be added on to, how reliable is it, and how good are their technicians? The best way to check is through references. If there are neighbors in your area who use a security system, they would be the best people to ask. As for an armed patrol, again a company that is established, one that has officers who are trained in all aspects of law enforcement including doing background investigations. Again, by driving around your area, the prospective owner will find people who already use a patrol service, they will have signs displayed in their front yards. Make sure whoever it is, that they are a twenty-four hour service, and that they work well with the police. An inspection of the company's facilities, communications, and other departments is also important.

As you can see an above average security system is a good idea, but it is also up to you to make sure that you can defend yourself before help arrives. Self defense courses such as Judo, Karate, and a variety of other martial arts are great exercise and often enjoyable to learn, but there are two drawbacks. One, the obvious disadvantage, is no one has devised a kick, scream or chop which can stop bullets. The other drawback is the physical limitations. Few ever master the art to the extent that they can not be overcome by a violent, stronger, perhaps insane, assailant. Also, many of the various forms of martial arts are ineffective when the person desiring to use this skill is crowded. When crowded you have little or no leverage, and the instant a desperate criminal has the advantage there are no second chances.

Mace is another overrated defense method. According to police statistics it is ineffective against anyone who is intoxicated or under the influence of drugs. The biggest problem is the type the average citizen is allowed to legally buy is a watered down version which is far less effective than the mace used by the police. If an attacker is wearing glasses, it will have little or no effect at all. Another problem with this method is you have to be dangerously close to an attacker to use the spray and a darn good shot to hit the attacker square in the eyes. More often than not mace will infuriate an attacker more than it will deter him.

There are other highly touted deterrents. You have key chains with special attachments, whistles, rings, and a variety of other odds and ends with a limit as to their practical application. Whether or not they are better than nothing depends on your attacker. If it works, great, if it doesn't you are at his mercy, possibly the mercy of a criminal who is madder than hell by now.

Our final comment about the multitude of devices now being sold, **BE CAREFUL!** We have seen the most absurd things on the market, mostly sold through mail order companies. They have many different descriptions of these devices, but the fact is, they aren't as powerful as they claim. If they were the police would be using them, and you probably wouldn't be allowed to buy them. It must be quite a shock to the person who has used these devices, and found they didn't disable their assailant, just made him mad! **Don't ever depend on a defensive weapon you have not been trained to use, or which has not been tested and proven to be reliable.**

When considering the variety of security systems we have discussed keep this in mind, if you have any of these systems, they do have some merit, though it may be limited; so don't jump on the phone and ask for a refund. They have value in that they will deter some criminals. The kind of criminal which alarms, dogs, and security windows would persuade to find another victim, for the most part, probably would not murder you. There are burglars who would prefer to rob your next door neighbor's house or car which is not equipped with a security system. We are talking in terms of the criminal who will end your life. In these situations you need the ultimate defense, the handgun. There is nothing else that has the flexibility of the handgun to defend and save your life in a deadly serious confrontation. The bottom line comes down to this, in a

19

life or death situation the handgun is the best choice, and we will thoroughly cover our reasons for recommending the handgun.

A graphic demonstration of the handgun's capabilities in the hands of a Combat Master. Seven shots have been fired and the camera has caught the spent cases still in the air. Even at this speed, all the shots are kept in the "vital zone" of the target.

20

CHAPTER 2

WHY THE HANDGUN — MYTH VERSUS FACT

When discussing the handgun for self defense we are talking about a life threatening situation, a time when you will find yourself facing an extremely violent criminal. Obviously, the handgun is the only realistic solution when compared to alternatives such as mace, locks, barking dogs and the like. You may be asking yourself why not a rifle or a shotgun? There are many advantages of a handgun over a rifle or a shotgun. We are not manufacturers of the handgun, our reasons are totally objective.

We feel that high powered rifles are absolutely unacceptable for self defense. They are basically offensive weapons, primarily designed for hunting big game or war like combat. They are designed for long range shooting and as a result can be dangerous to your family occupying other rooms in the home and even your neighbors. A bullet from this type of weapon can go through an attacker's body, through a wall or even into another home next to yours. Also, in many cases, it will only give you a one shot opportunity in spite of its load capacity. The reason for this is that when long range rifles are shot inside the noise from the echoing blast is so intense that it will not only affect your hearing in such a way that you will not be able to hear for a few seconds, but can also have a disorientating effect. If your attacker is aware of your disadvantage, he will have enough time to return fire taking full advantage of the situation. Self defense means never having to say you're sorry to an innocent party or to yourself!

Many people keep a .22 rifle around the house. They are inexpensive to purchase and very accurate, but they have several problems. Like the high powered rifle, the bullet from a .22 rifle can travel for over a mile. Unless you are an excellent marksman, the stopping power of the .22 is not very reliable. Rifles, in general, are awkward in the close combat situations you are most likely be involved. To shoot and aim properly, you will have to expose more of yourself than with the handgun. Because of its length there is the likelihood that as you aim around a doorway or a corner that the gun will be wrestled away from you by an attacker. With that in mind, the positions and angles you can accurately shoot from will be greatly limited.

The shotgun is, of course, a lethal weapon but it also has its limitations. Like the rifle it is difficult to handle in close quarters. Its blast can also be deafening and disorientating. A one or two shot shotgun is totally unacceptable. You have no way of knowing just how many intruders there might be. If there are more than one or two, you have had it. If there is only one intruder and you miss when you shoot the answer is the same. A shotgun can also be wrestled away from you the same as a rifle.

There are many myths concerning the effectiveness of the handgun that must be cleared up for you to understand the necessities of the procedures outlined in the other chapters. The majority of myths have been created by television and movie producers who, in their desire to have the most dramatic scenes possible, have created many dangerous attitudes concerning the handgun's application. Let's take a look at a couple of samples that we feel typify these almost comical attitudes.

Many of you might remember the original FBI television series with the leading character of Lew Erskin played by Efrem Zimbalist Jr. We used to watch this show regularly and had nicknamed his character "One Shot Lew." We remember one particular scene in which "One Shot Lew" was armed with a two inch .38 revolver. He jumped out of his black Ford sedan, ran down a hill and on another hill, directly across from him, a good two hundred yards, was the criminal armed with a high powered rifle taking aim and trying to shoot him. Lew, with one hand, took out the assailant with one shot. It was an unrealistic shot and quite impossible, as you will find out when you learn about the effective range of the two inch .38 revolver.

The long range accuracy, portrayed in dramas, is a myth. Another myth is that a bullet from a handgun can send someone flying through the air. To have enough force and power to do that, the recoil from a handgun would have to send the person firing it flying, too. Unless the first shot is an instant kill, more than likely, it will take two shots from any handgun to stop an attacker.

Another myth is the one we see on Westerns. The myth of disarming an attacker with one shot. First of all, most of the actual shootings during the time of the old West were cold blooded assassinations not the high noon duels we see on television. We doubt that anyone would have tried to only disarm an attacker. You would want to stop an attack

A frightening example of how easily a long gun (in this case a shotgun) is controlled and neutralized by an attacker.

23

and wouldn't waste precious time and ammunition trying to only disarm him, even if you were such a highly skilled marksman that could possibly disarm an attacker at that distance.

After reading this book and then practicing shooting at a range, you will realize how ridiculous Hollywood portrayals of the capabilities of a handgun are presented. It will provide you with a great many more laughs than you now enjoy while watching the gun slinging heroes on television and movies. With producer's multi-million dollar budgets for the purpose of "authenticity," it is amazing that they can't portray the handgun as it really is! Here are some facts about handguns.

1. Handguns do not go off by themselves.
2. Handguns are lethal weapons.
3. Handguns are dangerous in the hands of someone who has not been properly trained in their use.
4. Handguns have, for self defense, an effective realistic range of about fifty yards in the hands of an experienced individual.
5. Handguns do not cause accidental shootings.
6. Handguns are easily concealable and this is one of their greatest attributes.
7. Not all handguns are good for self defense.
8. Handguns are the best choice for self defense.
9. Most handguns are very well made.
10. Almost anyone can learn to effectively use a handgun.

There is nothing "macho" about a handgun. Unfortunately many women view handguns as part of a supposed "man's world." Our experience, in our ISI self defense training courses indicates that more and more women are turning to the handgun for self protection. Female enrollment in our classes is steadily increasing and interestingly enough we have found that women pick up the proper techniques for shooting faster than most men. Also, if a woman puts her mind to it, there is virtually no handgun we recommend that she can not learn to shoot well. The only limitations may be her hand size. This problem can be easily corrected by a simple modification of the grip on the handgun.

Women, statistically, have a much greater liklihood that they will become a victim of a violent crime as compared to men. Women need effective self defense techniques every bit as much and maybe even more than men. One of the main reasons for this is that obviously most sex related crimes are committed against women. Sex crimes against men usually involve the very young. Also, women are viewed by the criminal as more vulnerable and therefore a preferred choice over men.

If you live in Morton Grove, Illinois or San Francisco and their gun control laws have made you feel secure, you are living in a dream world. Handguns can easily be homemade, concealed and are sold illegally every day. Criminals aren't law abiding citizens and laugh at gun control laws. If they voted, they would vote for gun control to help make their lives safe from armed potential victims. Even if we banned all manufacturing of handguns, criminals would still have the capability of making one themselves or purchasing one illegally. If gun control laws were aimed at the criminal and not at the honest citizen's rights, as guaranteed by the constitution, we would be all for it. But, unfortunately, they aren't effective against the criminal and are nothing but rhetoric. Illegal handguns come in all sizes, shapes and forms, from hollowed out cigarette lighters to a cane a so-called blind man used. Obviously the illegal handgun can be difficult to identify, another good reason for assuming the worst.

A modern handgun is a precision, lethal weapon. It is a mechanical device which does not have a mind of its own. They do not go off by themselves! Accidental shootings are caused by the carelessness of an individual not by the gun. You can take a loaded semi-automatic pistol, cock it with the safety off and leave it untouched in the Smithsonian Institute and a thousand years from now it will not have discharged.

Handguns are dangerous when in the hands of anyone who has not been properly trained in their use. There are too many people, who have justifiably purchased a handgun for their own protection but, who fail to realize a basic mistake. They have never shot the weapon! Many don't even know how to use it. Some fire it but are not expert enough in the handling and applications of a handgun for self defense. These people have a choice. Either get rid of the gun or learn how to use it properly. These individuals have deluded themselves and actually have no protection until they resign themselves to taking the time to learn how to use their handguns.

Unlike television and the movies, handguns have an effective range of about fifty yards. However, most self defense shootings take place within a ten foot range. This fact is substantiated by police statistics. Most self defense situations, whether inside the home or outside, will fall into this range. This should give you another reason why we recommend the handgun over the rifle or shotgun. In this close of a range, the rifle or shotgun have no advantages over the handgun. They only have disadvantages in comparison.

Handguns do not cause accidental shootings, careless people do. A mistake with a handgun is irreversible. If it is negligently fired, you can only pray that no one is killed or injured. The child or the irresponsible adult who finds a gun and causes an "accident" is the fault of the owner who failed to properly secure the weapon in a safe place.

Not all handguns are good for self defense. We have outlined which types of handguns we recommend in another chapter. Some calibers are too small to be really effective and some use too powerful ammunition to be used easily and accurately. Your choice of

Typical modern double action revolver. Pictured is a Ruger .357 2¾'' barrel round butt. An excellent choice for a defensive handgun.

ammunition will make a definite difference in your ability to survive a lethal confrontation.

Handguns have many advantages. First, they are easy to get into quick action. Time is of the essence in a self defense situation, split seconds often making the difference between survival and extinction. They offer ease of mobility. You can carry one holstered or in one hand and have no limits as far as getting yourself positioned in a good defensive manner.

They allow for maximum concealability. They can be easily hidden and secured in places around the house where a burglar or child will not find them, as well as some irresponsible adult. You can carry them on your person completely concealed. This can be very important in many situations. For instance, you are a woman alone in the house and a repairman comes to the door. Chances are nothing would happen but, this particular man could be one of those individuals with sexual problems. He might at some time try to use force on you and a handgun could be kept in your pocket or one of the many holsters we will discuss. It would be awkward to let the repairman into your home while having to carry around a visible rifle or shotgun and expect the person to stay very long or even be willing to stay long enough to fix anything.

If you did have to use your handgun, there isn't as much danger to others in the house or to your neighbors as there are with long guns. The handgun has effective stopping power without the problem of over penetration. Handguns carry from five to sixteen rounds and can be quickly reloaded. Training and practicing with a handgun is much easier and won't punish you with an intense recoil like a shotgun or rifle will and in general the ammunition for practicing is cheaper than the ammunition for long guns.

The handgun is the only way an eighty-five year old woman can gain quick control of a two hundred pound young male attacker. It is the great equalizer. Although we try to prepare you for the worst in this book, in many cases, the presence of the handgun will act as a deterrent putting **you,** the responsible citizen, in control of a potentially violent situation.

If you can walk and chew gum at the same time, you can learn to accurately shoot a handgun. You will need the physical use of at least one hand, reasonably good vision, corrected or otherwise, an average amount of hand/eye coordination and in general the normal physical capabilities of the average person. If you can drive a car, learning how to use those simple controls, you have the ability to learn how to shoot a handgun.

The skills required for self defense shooting are basic skills. We are not saying that anyone can become a champion in professional shooting competitions but, if you have the desire to learn, anyone can learn to shoot well enough to defend him or herself.

In our opinion, the finest "big bore" automatic pistol ever manufactured is Colt's Government model in 45 ACP. Properly modified and in trained hands it's the ultimate defensive handgun.

28

When we speak of the hand/eye coordination needed for defensive shooting, we simply mean learning to use your arms and hands as an extension of your eyes, while at the same time, developing the ability to quickly bring your hands holding the weapon on target and delivering an accurate shot. With practice and training your hands and arms will respond to what your eyes are looking at and will automatically raise to a position where you can deliver an accurate shot. In a self defense situation your response must become automatic. This is critical to your survival.

The right attitude to become an effective shooter is the willingness to spend a certain amount of time practicing. A reasonable commitment is all you really need, as most people will find they improve with practice. When you first start out you will notice the most dramatic improvement mainly because you may have none or very little experience and no bad habits to break. You will rapidly gain an understanding of the techniques and progress quickly. The more you shoot, the more your skills will increase. What we are striving to teach is confidence and efficiency for self defense purposes. You don't have to worry about acquiring the skill of a world class champion shooter at this point, although you may want to try for that later.

We have taught a great many people in our ISI Self Defense courses and have noticed that people with no experience with guns usually have one or the other idea about what shooting a handgun is all about. Some are very intimidated by handguns, others think that they are as easy as pie to use and have embraced the Hollywood portrayals. They soon find out that neither attitude is accurate. We talked with two women who recently took our class before and afterwards. Laura had the idea that handguns were a snap to use and Sharon was fearful about the whole idea.

Q. What made you decide to take this class?
S. Well, living in a big city I figured that I'd better find a better way to protect myself than just wishing for the best.
L. Some friends of mine took your course and told me it was a lot of fun so I decided to give it a try.
Q. Have either of you ever fired a handgun before?
S. No, I've fired a .22 rifle before but never a handgun.
L. Me either but I've taken a class on using Mace. That stuff just didn't seem like it would really stop someone who was intent on hurting you plus I always wondered what would happen if the wind was blowing in my direction. You can't ask someone who is attacking you to change places because of the wind.
Q. Both of you will be using .38 revolvers?
S. Yes. I keep telling myself that I'm probably just scaring myself about how powerful the kick on these things are, but I'm still kind of nervous about using one of these.

L. I'm not worried about this gun kicking but it is a lot heavier than I expected. They look so small to feel this heavy. I don't know much about handguns but I doubt that they have any kick. They're just too small.

Q. They really don't have that much kick or recoil, as we call it. What makes you think that they have a lot of recoil?

S. I guess just some things that I've seen on T.V. I've seen something where they have shown police officers practicing at one of those indoor ranges and they always seem like they would kick because every time one of them fired his gun his hands seemed to fly up.

Q. Try making a fist with your left hand and push it into your right palm with your arms extended. I'm going to give a little shove against your hands.

S. That's what the kick is like? That's nothing. Now all I have to worry about is whether or not I can shoot straight. Wait a minute, what about the recoil if you can only use one hand?

Q. It will be the same. We will start off showing you how to shoot using both hands and when you get comfortable with that we will show you how easy it is to use just one hand. We are going to teach you how to stand so that your body will absorb most of the recoil not just your arms.

S. My left hand is a lot weaker than my right. What if I don't have the strength?

Q. You will probably be surprised when you find that you can handle one handed shooting with your left hand as well as your right hand. The only problem that some people have with their left hand, mainly with the revolver, is that they can't always pull the trigger at first. But, with practice, they overcome this. If you have this problem, you will just have to build up the muscles in your left hand.

S. That's true. I really wouldn't want to be in the position where I had to use only my left hand and then find out that I had a problem pulling the trigger.

Q. Now that you two have finished the course what do you think?

L. On top of having sore muscles?

Q. The more that you practice the easier it will get. You've been using muscles that you normally don't for the last two days and they are bound to get a little sore at first.

L. Well, I really used to think that handguns weren't much more than toys. I've got a lot more respect for them now. It's nice to know that I could use one of these to defend myself and really know what I'm doing. I'm glad that I didn't have to use one before I took this course. I wouldn't have had any idea of what to do. It's really amazing what I thought about handguns and what I think now. I thought you could just go out and buy one and that was all there was to it. Now I know that there's more to using a handgun to defend yourself than just owning one.

S. I've got to admit that I had myself all worked up over nothing. I was expecting it to really kick and it didn't have much kick at all. Unlike Laura, I thought that handguns were really complicated and hard to use. Besides finding out that it wasn't as bad as I expected, I feel like I can take care of myself and use a handgun if I have to. I did learn a few things that I hadn't thought about as far as safety goes, like how to safely load and unload and double check to make sure the gun isn't loaded and about pointing it in a safe direction.

L. One thing I definitely learned is that I need a lot more practice before I would even think about calling myself a decent shooter.

S. I really enjoyed myself. I wouldn't mind going to a range on a regular basis to practice. It was a lot of fun.

Many women in today's society must rely on themselves for protection. The handgun is the "equalizer." This armed and trained 110-pound woman is capable of stopping a violent attack, no matter how large or strong the assailant might be.

CHAPTER 3

WOMEN AND SELF DEFENSE

Statistics of violent crimes show that the criminal sees women in a disadvantaged light as weak, easy targets. As a result, women are particularly susceptible and vulnerable when it comes to crimes of a violent nature. Unfortunately, many women read magazines, watch talk shows, and are influenced by a variety of other media into having a false sense of security by the unrealistic approaches to self defense which are touted. They are told that ineffective methods such as mace, customized key chains, whistles and the like can save their lives. Rarely, if ever, have we heard women being told to use a handgun. It's as if women were being told that they shouldn't go to such an extreme to protect their lives but, instead, should use a more "lady-like" and thoroughly ineffective method. It is necessary for women in today's society to overcome this dangerous brainwashing and stand up for their right to use the only really effective means of protecting themselves, the handgun. Unquestionably no violent criminal is going to compliment you on what a polite victim you were.

Squeamishness is an acquired characteristic which makes many women shy away from using a handgun, particularly in the case of self defense where they may be forced to take the life of another to save their own. Most women are not taught, as young girls, to defend themselves. Instead they are taught to depend on someone else. At the very least, they are taught to run from danger when there isn't a man to turn to for protection. Women are also taught, subconsciously, that guns are in the exclusive domain of men. Handguns are designed for self defense and to be used by anyone. Guns have always been presented as powerful and dangerous. There are many examples of powerful and dangerous sports and occupations which, for the most part, have been considered the domain of men. In recent years, women have entered into many sports and business occupations formerly considered only for men. Some have done well and others have excelled. Handguns are no exception. There is no reason why any woman can not learn to be proficient, not only in the use of a handgun, but also in their own capabilities to defend themselves if they were ever attacked.

There will be some women who will respond to this statement by saying that by our advocating the use of a handgun for self defense we are teaching them to kill. What they are really saying is that they would rather choose to be a dead pacifist rather than a survivor. With this kind of attitude, they had better hope they are never faced with a life or death situation because chances are they will be killed. No matter what we tell anyone with this attitude, they will insist that they would rather be killed than possibly have to kill someone who is willing and able to kill them. Obviously, the choice is yours, **if** you are the only one who would be affected. Many households in this country are headed by women with children. The point is simple. If you have children, you also must consider their lives if you are ever attacked.

Many women have shied away from even considering using the handgun because of its portrayal on television as a weapon with a tremendous amount of "kick" known as recoil. They, naturally, think it would take a great deal of strength to handle a weapon like this. **This is not true.** The only limitation some women might find is the grip size of a handgun as it comes equipped from the factory. Most handguns can be inexpensively modified to suit individual needs. The recoil on recommended handguns is light to moderate, not the shocking recoil pictured by Hollywood.

If you have children in your home, you are probably concerned about the danger of bringing a gun into the house. We cover safety in detail in this book. However, when you assume the responsibility to own a handgun it is also **your** responsibility to follow all safety procedures outlined in this book including how, where and when to safely store it. The handgun will not be a danger in a household with a safety conscious gun owner. Just as you would safeguard against and educate your child about the danger of drain cleaners, you must also do so with a handgun.

To most of you this probably sounds pretty good so far. You are, hopefully, accepting the fact that handguns can be handled by women and that when safety rules are observed and followed they can be safe even when there are children in the house. There is one last thing to think about. "How will I react to a life and death situation." You don't know; no one does. The fact is (excuse what may appear to be chauvinism) that men are more accustomed to handling threats and fighting. Few men went through school without at least one fist fight. It is, sad to say, the way men deal with most situations that effect their pride. Most women do not have this experience. Some women fear that they would freeze with fear and not be able to pull the trigger if they had to, and the gun would then become useless in their hands.

We'd like to point out an appropriate analogy. A high percentage of pedestrians who are hit by cars had the time to get out of the way or at least jump on the hood of an oncoming car but didn't. They had the time but when they saw the car and realized they were in trouble they froze. This can happen to an individual who isn't properly prepared for a life threatening situation. One of us personally witnessed a case where a person who was trained in CPR was present when a man had a heart attack and stopped breathing. It appeared the man who had the training stopped breathing also, and he froze and forgot everything he had learned. Fortunately, a strong shake by his wife jogged his memory and the ending was a happy one for all concerned. His first aid training was limited in that it didn't include the psychological aspects of being the one and only available person to save someone's life and this almost cost someone his life. Your self defense training outlined in this book does include the psychological training for this type of situation, and we specifically give you what you need to know and think about daily to be mentally prepared. Mental preparations must be practiced just like regular target practice.

It is now a scientifically proven fact that women are basically more intuitive than men. Intuition itself may serve as an early warning system, but when in a life or death situation don't mistake guessing for intuition.

According to statistics, women are much more susceptible to sex related assaults than men. On occasion, men are raped but such an assault is extremely rare compared to sexual assaults against women. More and more we are seeing a great increase in female enrollment in our Self Defense training courses. We are not going to attempt here to explain the reasons for the increase in sex related crimes against women. The reason why you could become a victim is something the legislators have been toying with for years. The fact is that these crimes happen and seem to be occurring more frequently and as a woman you may need to be proficient in the use of a handgun more than most men. You are vulnerable because the criminal thinks you are. How many women do you know who have been harassed, at some time, while driving, walking down the street or by an obscene phone call? Most of you probably have been harassed at least once. It may seem that to be a woman you have to tolerate this abuse. Unfortunately with weak laws you do, but you do not have to tolerate being assaulted. You have to assume the worst at all times. What seems to be a harmless cat call could turn out to be a warning of real trouble. Any harassment should ring an alarm in your head. You should be prepared to act should the individual who made this remark indeed be sick and a danger to you. Always proceed with caution in any situation of this type. Almost every woman we know has received an obscene phone call. They are alarming and for very good reason. It does not matter what statistics the phone companies provide showing that many of these calls are nothing more than pranks if you are the one who ends up paying the price.

Some people like to look at the world through rose colored glasses and say "what a wonderful place this world would be if there were no guns." Where their illogical idealism fails is that in the reality of today's society, the person who is the biggest and strongest brute will still have you at his mercy. The handgun eliminates that problem because it serves as the great equalizer. It makes up for what strength you lack physically.

Women can learn at a young age how to use the handgun and thus be ready and capable to defend their life or the life of another.

Women tend not to have the same awareness and tolerance for violence as men. They prefer to avoid confrontations and have no desire to take up boxing. However, many women have made the decision that they are tired of being a potential victim. When it comes to self defense, men have a much more aggressive attitude than most women. If you have a tendency to hesitate, you must overcome this. It is not enough to just purchase a handgun. You must mentally prepare yourself for an actual situation through the use of mind games and practice, practice, practice. To give you an example of mind games, picture yourself in your living room and envision an attacker breaking down your door. Now determine if you have a lethal confrontation on your hands and what your next step will be. The first thing you will do is to get into a barricaded position and identify the target. The instant that you are convinced that you are being lethally threatened and have sighted your target you are going to have to fire. There is a difference between men and women when it comes to justification of why and when you use a handgun for self defense. A woman has a legitimate fear for her life when confronted by an unarmed two hundred pound man because this man could actually beat her to death. A man, facing his equal, does not have this same degree of legitimate fear. This doesn't mean that a woman can shoot anyone who vaguely threatens her, only that she doesn't have to wait as long to establish imminent danger as a man would. It boils down to the bigger the disparity in size the sooner the justification. The importance of training is very evident when discussing this aspect. You must know how to use your gun and when to use it. Training will also help you to develop a calmness and confidence when faced with a pressure situation. Learning the correct steps for self defense will help you overcome panic if you are ever faced with a life or death situation.

Many people have made the mistake of thinking that just having a gun will do the trick whether or not it's loaded. This fallacy could cost you your life. You will not have the time to load your gun when faced with an immediate and close range lethal threat. That is not the time to think about loading your weapon. Proficiency with a gun is absolutely necessary if you expect to be able to defend yourself. Owning a gun you have never fired and have never practiced with is the same as keeping it unloaded. You may be able to fire it but chances are you will lack the accuracy to use it effectively. If you are going to own a handgun, **learn how to use it.**

Many women have been attacked while away from their homes, in their cars, parking lots, leaving work, etc. There are purses designed especially for carrying a weapon. They are designed with purse snatching in mind so that you will not be left defenseless and with an obvious criminal now in possession of a gun. Women need to carry guns for self protection more than anyone for the obvious reason that they are seen as easy targets by criminals. We all try to avoid high crime areas but there are times when you may have to go into such an area or when you may be faced with the unexpected in an otherwise safe area. There are many types of violent crimes, specifically rape, where if more women did carry a weapon there would be less inclination on the part of a would-be rapist to attack a lone woman. We're sure that had assaulted women fired on their attackers instead of being defenseless, eventually a strong reduction of attacks would result. A criminal purposely seeks out easy victims, not those who fight back.

If you carry a gun in your car, keep it on your person. Never leave your gun unattended! Gun ownership carries with it the responsibility that you never allow your gun to fall into the wrong hands. When driving alone, you must be aware that there are people who will either force you off the road or try to trick you into leaving the road and getting out of your car. One of the most common tricks is honking and pointing at your car as if something's wrong. Another is someone purposely bumping your car so you will pull over and get out to inspect the damage and exchange insurance information. Never pull over in an isolated area. Drive to a well lighted area before you get out of your car such as a police station, a fire station or a gas station with lots of people around. If you are stranded or have to stop somewhere, don't get out of your car except momentarily to raise the hood of your car to indicate trouble. If someone comes up to your car, talk to them through a slightly lowered window. Don't get out. You can exchange insurance information through a window or ask someone to call a tow truck. There is no reason for you to leave the safety of your car. Never show your weapon to anyone who approaches your car. You could not only scare an innocent person but also tip off an attacker and lose the advantage of surprise. If an attacker finds you are armed, he can easily pull out his own gun. Wait until he has broken your window and is actually reaching into the car before you show your weapon. This is an important advantage and you need every advantage you can get at this point.

Awareness is probably your biggest advantage and the one most people don't practice enough. How many times have you casually parked your car and gotten out without taking the time to look around? How many times have you left your car unlocked because you "will only be gone a minute?" Do you always look at the back seat before you get into your car? Small steps like these could not only save your life but could also help you to avoid the need to use your gun. Your gun is your last line of defense and you can help avoid the need to use it by taking a few precautions. Awareness is the number one key to survival. You should always be aware of your surroundings and take all necessary precautions to safeguard yourself. The one thing that we see so often are people who appear to be fumbling for their keys. You should always have your keys out and ready. Try to avoid walking around in a daze.

We've seen too many people who walk right by blind doorways without seeming to notice them or for that matter much of anything about their surroundings. Pay attention to your surroundings! A little paranoia is a good thing. You will never have the time to react effectively if you are not aware until it's too late.

More and more women are realizing the handgun's value for self-protection and are refusing to become another victim of violent crime.

Awareness and the determination to survive an attack will give you a much better chance. Those women who own a handgun and have learned how to use it have made the decision to survive. The following interview is with a woman we feel illustrates both the need for women to own handguns as well as the ease with which the average woman can learn to use a handgun effectively. Susan is a twenty-four year old, single, attractive law school graduate who served her clerkship at a District Attorney's Office in a large city.

Q. What were some of your functions with the D.A.'s Office?
S. Basically I worked with the Hardcore Gang Unit. This was the division that investigates and prosecutes all gang related incidents and unfortunately most of them involved murder. Everyday there seemed to be some type of gang related incident. Sometimes they were crimes committed between gangs, often involving the murder of an innocent bystander and of course there were murders that were committed for the sole purpose of murder, which were probably the most frightening.
Q. Why did you find those the most frightening?
S. There was no motive other than to kill.
Q. Were these random murders done within their particular area?
S. No, not at all. They could happen anywhere. There was a spell, last year, when they picked out a very nice suburban area and, quite simply, murdered people. It is worse within their own area of course, but I found it quite frightening that they did not hesitate to go into areas such as where I live where the last thing you would expect to have to worry about would be gang related murders. It is actually a very prestigious thing for them among their peers. They call it being a "shooter." When they do kill someone, they get a tatoo with a gun and a hand on their arm. I was able to go on a **"ride along"** program with a police unit in a high crime area and to put it simply it is unbelievable. The gang members ride around with guns in their car ready to do battle with another gang or just rob or kill on a whim. On one of the rides with the police they stopped a car with five gang members, ran a check on them after finding guns and found that one of them was wanted for murder.
Q. How old was he?
S. Very young, an eleven year old, for instance, was arrested and found guilty of rape. They literally grow up with the morals and ethics, if you can call them that, as prescribed by the gang in their area. Needless to say, at such a young age they are taught that life means nothing and they believe it.
Q. So they think nothing of going into a nice suburban area and robbing or killing?
S. What they think is that they can do anything they want anywhere

they want and they do. It doesn't matter whether you live in a city like New York with subways or a city with freeways, these gangs are very mobile and the high risk factor of going into the more lucrative areas does not even make them hesitate.

Q. Do they have a somewhat ruthless nature?

S. Well, yes and no. When you talk to them alone they are very much afraid, after all most of them are so young. Well, they are just children. When they are together in a group it is a totally different thing. They are ruthless. In order to be accepted you have to be rough, you have to have a gun and to be respected, you have to kill.

Q. Are they out committing crimes such as burglaries to make money?

S. Yes, of course, but sadly there always seems to be a murder involved.

Q. The more experience you had with these gangs, did you become frightened with their ruthlessness and their lack of value for human life?

S. Absolutely. I guess the best example, something that really shook me, was when, during a court case in which a gang member was being tried for murder, other members of the gang would go to the court out of curiosity. They were very callous toward the law, they had no fear or respect for the law at all. Regardless of the sentence pronounced on their friend it seemed to have no impact on them. Part of getting caught was going to prison and I suppose that this too added to their prestige.

Q. What about girls? Were they in these gangs?

S. Oh they were in the gangs, had the same values. They carried knives and other weapons, but I didn't see or hear of any who carried guns, which of course doesn't mean they wouldn't. It certainly doesn't mean they wouldn't use one.

Q. Now, you live in a nice suburban neighborhood, a good twenty miles from any high crime area. Do you feel far enough away from all the crime to be secure at least from gang activities?

S. Well, it isn't constantly on my mind but then again it wouldn't surprise me. The frightening thing is the type of criminal element they represent. First of all, the chances of something happening where I live, of being one of their victims, is very small. But, if it should happen to me, the odds in being in my favor wouldn't matter anymore. Secondly, I think most people like to go into a city area from time to time to enjoy the things a city offers and it is quite simply very dangerous because of gangs and other types of criminals within the city. I find it hard to enjoy myself knowing these people are out there ready to rape, rob, murder or anything else they might feel like doing.

Q. You have had your own problem with criminals also?

S. Yes, I have. Over the summer I was living alone. About 10:00 PM, one night, my dog, who was tied up out back, started barking. I thought maybe something was around. Then I noticed there was a car out in front of the house. In the neighborhood I live, well, I knew it didn't belong. The houses are spread quite far apart and it was the only car out there. I then walked from the back bedroom to the front of the house and saw the headlights of the car. Then I saw someone shining a flashlight through the living room drapes. So I jumped back and ran into the bedroom and phoned the police. As I went to the telephone, I heard whoever it was trying to break in through the kitchen window. I was having a problem getting the police and as I was trying to do this I heard them take off the kitchen screen. Finally I got through to the police and I told them someone was breaking into my house right now, through a window, and that I was alone. He asked me if I could get out of the house, but I couldn't because of where I was situated. He then told me to make noise and that if he was just there to rob he would leave. I then turned the stereo on full blast. I was in total hysterics at the time and was just cowering in a corner, crying. I didn't know who it was, how many there were or what they might do to me, and I had no way to defend myself at all. Fortunately, the stereo scared him off and when I heard him climb back out the window I ran to the front of the house to try and get the license plate number. It was too dark and I couldn't read the numbers.

Q. This panicked feeling you talked about, do you think it could have been avoided if you had thought beforehand about what you would do if something like this happened?

S. That's hard to answer. My father told me all my life to think about what I would do if something like this ever happened. Well, I didn't because I just never thought it would happen. About the only way I prepared was that I just felt if something did happen I would be able to keep calm and deal with it without fear and panic.

Q. After this happened did you go out and purchase a gun?

S. No, at first I thought about living with someone else, getting a security system, getting another dog and more locks. I felt very defenseless but really thought about all the alternatives to owning a gun. Part of the problem was that in studying to be an attorney I was worried about carrying a gun illegally, getting caught and not being able to practice law. I eventually came to the conclusion that I couldn't practice law if someone killed me.

Q. Did you think about studying a martial art like judo or using Mace as an alternative?

S. Oh, I took Karate and I realized real quick that if I had to get so close to someone to use it I really wouldn't have a chance. The only women I saw who would even have a chance were those who were blackbelts and studied all their lives to perfect their skill. It just doesn't seem practical to me for women and most men to study a martial art for self defense against the kinds of criminals that are out there unless they devote years to learning it but in the meantime what do they do?

Q. What about Mace?

S. I took a Mace class as well. A month or so after the class I took out my can of Mace to show a girlfriend how to use it and it didn't work. I thought that was great. I had been carrying it around for protection, jogging, going out at night and it wouldn't have worked. I really don't feel it is a very reliable method of defense.

Q. Did these failures of alternative forms of defense make you decide to get a gun?

S. Well, that was a factor but another incident was what really made up my mind. I was driving home after work, it was still daylight and I was on a country road where there is very little traffic and a car came up on me from behind and seemed to be trying to pass me. About three times he started to pass me then just stayed in the passing lane even with me. Then I started to panic, thinking that this person was trying to run me off the road. Things like this happen so fast, well, you have time to react, but you certainly don't have the time to think things out if you're not prepared for it. There wasn't a shoulder on this road, just stopping areas every few miles apart. Finally, when I came to one, I pulled into it to give him the benefit of the doubt, and then there was no longer any doubt. He pulled in right behind me. I then pulled out and it became like a drag race. I was hoping it was just kids playing a sick joke. At the next pullout I pulled in part way, trying to outsmart him, but I guess he figured that out because he pulled directly in front of me, blocking my car. Then the man on the passenger side jumped out and ran behind my car so I couldn't leave. My doors were both locked but my windows were open part way. I rolled up my window and closed the vent. By the time I went to the passenger side window one of the men had put his fingers in the window and I couldn't move the crank. I really thought they had me at that point. He was trying to get the window down and why he couldn't I don't know. He then stuck his face in the window and started screaming at me that "nice people don't call the police." He sounded deranged and I really felt, if they got me, I was as good as dead. The one guy was behind the car but, for some reason, I didn't think about hitting him. Anyway, I was able to back the car out and get away and for some reason they didn't follow me anymore.

Q. If this happened to you again what would you do?

S. First of all, I would never stop or slow down and give them the opportunity to block me, and second of all, I wouldn't worry whether or not I was going to run one or both of them over. I would do whatever I had to to get away.

Q. Did this convince you that you needed a gun?

S. Oh yeah! There wasn't a doubt in my mind that it was the only way I could protect myself. To have two men try to attack me in the daytime, less than a mile from my home, made me realize that there just wasn't an alternative.

Q. I know what happened to you was very frightening and that in itself would make most of us consider getting a gun but were there any other contributing factors?

S. Well, I had a girlfriend who was raped. When a former roommate was home alone the house was broken into and luckily they only tied her up. It just doesn't seem that crime is a rare occurrence anymore. It seems that most of the honest population has been a victim of some type of crime or will be during their lifetime. Your survival depends on the whim of a criminal unless you protect yourself. A friend of mine recently was murdered outside a very nice, plush restaurant on the coast. There was no motive outside of the fact that the man who murdered him was harrassing his date, he interceded, talked the other man into leaving them alone, they shook hands and he was shot to death as he walked away.

Q. Did they catch the murderer?

S. They caught him by a stroke of luck.

Q. Did he have a prior record?

S. Yes, he had a number of convictions, once for shooting randomly into an occupied home.

Q. What was the feeling in the D.A.'s Office you worked in concerning the hardcore, repeat offenders?

S. A feeling of hopelessness. The juvenile could commit any crime, even murder, and would be released without any type of effective rehabilitation and as for adult criminals, we all know from statistics, our prison system is not protecting honest citizens from violent, unrehabilitated criminals.

Q. How about murder? What I'm getting at is do criminals try to avoid murdering someone during a robbery or would they just as soon get rid of any witnesses?

S. If they feel someone can testify against them or turn them in, that's what they think about. In other words, they don't question whether it's right or wrong to kill. They question what is best for them. They don't think of the consequences of the murder because, first, they don't think they'll get caught and second, if they do, they don't think they will be convicted and, three, if they are convicted they do not think they will be penalized very much for it.

Q. What type of handgun did you buy?

S. I bought a Smith and Wesson .38 snub-nose. It fits perfectly in my purse.

Q. Before you made the final decision to purchase this gun were you having any second thoughts?

S. Well, I always saw a gun as something that is very masculine. Now I think that's kind of foolish. Women probably need a gun for protection much more than men unless, of course, they want to make sure they have a man with them at all times. I just didn't want to live like that. I guess what scared me the most into actually doing it was that during the attempted burglary when I was home, the next day I discovered that they had disabled my car and cut off the outside lights. They really meant business and in spite of the so called macho appearance of a gun at least now I feel safe in that I can defend myself.

Q. Had you ever fired a handgun before you purchased your own?

S. No, I had shot a shotgun which was quite hard for me to handle the kick but not a handgun.

Q. Did someone teach you how to shoot?

S. Well, I went twice a week for three weeks with my brother who shoots and at some point I hope to get some professional instruction as well.

Q. Did you find it difficult to learn?

S. Not really. The first time I had a lot to learn and made a lot of mistakes but after that it was just like a tuning in process and in only a couple of hours I shot well enough to defend myself in the type of situations that would be involved in self defense. I still am improving, of course, and the better I get the better I feel.

Q. Before you actually shot the gun what did you expect?

S. I had visions of the kick from the gun overpowering me. I expected it to be very difficult to learn. In a way it was difficult but once I learned the basics it became easier and easier. As far as the kick and general handling of the gun I can't imagine anyone who is not crippled not having the strength to learn how to use the handgun to the point of shooting well enough to defend themselves. The thing that surprised me the most was when I went to practice at a local range I felt a little embarrassed being a woman going to shoot.

Q. Why?

S. I envisioned being the only woman there, surrounded by a group of masculine, tough looking men. I would say over half of the people there were women just like myself, probably there for the same reason.

Q. As you learned the basics and became comfortable with shooting did it also have a recreational aspect as well?

S. Yes. I would say it was fun. I've only shot at an indoor range but I'm looking forward to shooting at an outdoor range. I guess you could

45

say if I had to compare my Karate or Mace instruction to shooting there would be no comparison as far as it being fun rather than a chore.

Q. Do you feel a lot safer now that you know how to use a gun and keep one with you?

S. There is no way to describe the feeling of security you feel knowing you are not defenseless. That anyone, even a group of men, no matter how strong they are that now I'm on even turf with them if they were to try something. I know now if I'm in my home, and someone is breaking in, and the police tell me they can't get anyone out right away that I'm not at the mercy of the whim of some deranged individual. He can rob the house if he wants. I'm not going to hunt or challenge anyone but if he comes after me, I'm not going to let him do what he wants to do to me. I also think I carry myself differently now when I am out walking through a parking lot at night or wherever. Knowing I have a gun in my purse, many times with my hand on it, I don't have that look that criminals like to see.

Q. What look is that?

S. Well, most policemen will tell you that the way people carry themselves, such as appearing frightened or timid makes them more likely to be a victim. When you carry a gun and know how to use it, the fear and timidness just isn't there anymore. I think I project an image of someone who is not going to be an easy victim, and I think that is very important as a deterrent in itself.

Q. Have you had any problems since you started carrying a gun?

S. No, well at least no confrontations. There have been times when I've been glad I had it just in case.

Q. Do you think all women should carry a handgun?

S. That sounds radical but it really isn't. I think anyone who is responsible enough to properly care for the gun, takes it upon themselves to learn how to use it and is safety conscious should have a gun. I just don't see a choice, for women especially. It's sad but it's a fact of life, if you don't carry a gun or keep one for self defense, you could easily find yourself at the mercy of people who place no value on life.

CHAPTER 4

SAFETY

There is no such thing as being too safe with any type of firearm. It is an unfortunate truth that many "accidental" shootings occur with a presumed "unloaded firearm." There is no such thing as an accidental discharge, there are only negligent ones. Police reports are full of these "accidental shootings." A youngster finds his father's gun at home and fatally shoots himself or someone else, a person cleaning his gun is injured when the gun "accidentally" goes off. The list goes on and on. They are accidental only in that it was not intentional on the part of the person concerned. What it really means is that the death or injury was due to negligence!

The handgun is a mechanical device. For the gun to fire it must be loaded and the trigger and hammer must be activated by either an object or someone's finger. In short, the gun will not go off by itself. It has no mind, no eyes or soul with the capacity to forgive or be sorry. The gun only has mechanical reflexes which are activated by a series of manipulations. You do have a conscience and the physical and mental abilities to follow the safety guidelines at all times. **It is your responsibility.** If you do not take this aspect of self defense seriously, you should not own or ever use a gun of any type. Your conscience is of little help to someone you might have injured by not applying the proper safety procedures. The ultimate tragedy is a death or injury caused by an "accident" which was in someone's control and power to avoid. Every responsible individual involved in an accidental shooting will tell you what a horror it is to live with the knowledge that someone is dead because he was careless.

Firearms are **always** considered loaded and must be handled accordingly. It is considered rude and hazardous to handle firearms without total respect for their lethal capabilities. The safety procedures

One of the simplest ways to illustrate the destructive force of a handgun is to place cans of "shaken" carbonated soda on a post. (Top) Then from a safe distance with eye and ear protection for those watching, fire a shot and hit the cans. They will literally explode. (Bottom)

This vividly shows the type of power a handgun is capable of unleashing. This method is very good for children, but adults can learn something from it as well.

outlined are not only for you to follow but also to make you aware of how others around you should handle their firearms. If you are at some-body's house, at a target range or a gun store, and someone is not following the proper safety procedures, you should not hesitate to tell him. A common problem is the individual who waves the muzzle end of the firearm carelessly; threatening people in the potential target area of the muzzle. If any unsafe situation persists, **leave!** Under no circumstances should you tolerate this or put yourself in danger. It could save your life. Some of the worst gun handlers we have ever seen are those who should have obviously known better. Don't become a victim of someone else's negligence.

Never point a firearm at anything you are not willing to destroy. It does not matter how many times you have checked the chamber or cylinder or how sure you are the gun is unloaded. There are too many directions a gun can be pointed safely to ever take any chances. Too many adults let unsupervised children treat a gun like a toy. If you want to show off your new gun to a friend who is not familiar with the rules of safety, inform him of the proper procedures before handing him the firearm. Many cocktail parties have come to an abrupt end when some idiot decided to play with a gun and fatally injured someone. Educate those around you in the proper safety procedures, including your children.

Firearms ownership carries with it serious responsibilities! Children must be taught to understand guns and respect their lethal power.

If someone hands you a gun to look at or inspect, it is your responsibility to examine the firearm to be sure it is unloaded. This holds true regardless of whether the individual has checked it before handing it to you. When you hand it back to them, if they are following proper procedures they will recheck the gun again. It doesn't matter whether you hand the gun back and forth a dozen times, check it a dozen times. The reason is quite simple; safety. You will find it becomes reflex conditioning to automatically check a gun every time you pick one up.

Guns do not load themselves. But, we all have our lapses. "I forgot I loaded the gun" is a hell of an excuse after it is mishandled and a shot fired. By having a handgun for self defense, more often than not it will be stored loaded. Don't depend on your memory to determine this. Someone else in your house, who has access to the gun, might have loaded it and for some reason forgot to tell you. No one has the right to gamble a life based on their supposed inability to make an error.

A very common safety problem with the double action revolver occurs when the ejector rod is pushed to empty the cylinder and only four or five rounds fall out leaving one or two rounds still in the chambers. For safety's sake, always visually check each chamber and don't just count the rounds in your hand. It is too easy to make a mistake. If you count wrongly and don't check the chambers, when you close the cylinder and the trigger is actuated you could be in for a big surprise. You must visually check each chamber in the cylinder and make sure that each one is empty.

The most common mistake that people make with the semi-automatic is removing the live round from the chamber without first removing the magazine. The round that was taken out of the chamber has now been replaced by another round from the magazine and you still have a loaded pistol ready to discharge when the trigger is pulled. Many people who have made this mistake, but followed the safety procedure of never pointing the gun at anything they do not wish to destroy, have shot mirrors, carpets, TV sets, sofas and other miscellaneous replaceable items while practicing dry firing with a presumably unloaded gun. To avoid this problem, always remove the magazine first and then the chambered round from the pistol. Then open the action and visually inspect the chamber to be sure there isn't a cartridge in place. Then and only then do you "dry fire" the weapon.

When considering self defense, there is another area of safety which applies strictly to a life and death situation. This area of safety could also be known as reliability. It is obviously dangerous to depend upon a firearm which does not function properly or which is loaded with undependable ammunition. If, when practicing, you notice any problems at all with your firearm have it checked by a reliable gunsmith at once. Taking proper care of your gun is both a safety related necessity as well as an application of good common sense in taking care of a mechanical device in which you have invested money and time, not to mention its use as a life saving device.

A properly working handgun is naturally of little use without dependable ammunition. When you buy ammunition, let's say fifty rounds, you should inspect it and take about twenty rounds and fire it in the pistol intended for its use. If all goes well the remaining rounds can be kept for your self defense use. As a rule, this ammunition will be kept separate from the ammunition you use to practice with at the target range. One reason for separate ammunition is to insure that you don't use all your ammunition at the target range and then don't have any at home when you would most need it. How many times have we all forgotten to replace something? The other reason is that you will be using a different type of load to practice with to avoid undue wear on your handgun.

As far as storage goes, don't be fooled by supposed experts who fought in one of the great wars. Military ammunition is sometimes good for decades due to the fact that it was sealed in lacquer. Modern cartridges purchased over the counter have an advised shelf life of one year when properly stored. Most law enforcement agencies change their ammunition once a year. You can still use it for target practice and if it misfires or doesn't fire at least the target won't be shooting back.

When storing your ammunition, keep it in a cool dry place at normal room temperature to insure its reliability. Ammunition that is exposed to extreme heat or cold should be considered unusable for self defense purposes. Extreme cold, heat or moisture can create a chemical deterioration within the powder or primer, which is not visible, causing the ammunition to have irregular or no ignition. In a self defense situation, you can not say to an attacker, "time out, I need to reload!" If you ever have any doubt as to the possible reliability of your ammunition, use it for target practice.

Being human there is always a chance of an error resulting in an accidental discharge. Like driving a car, accidents do happen. You can't always point your car in a safe direction, but, as we have stated over and over, your gun can and always should be pointed in a safe direction. Whether you shoot a hole in your couch or floor or embarass yourself at the target range, the only injury will be to your pride and you will probably deserve it. But you will also be very relieved that you followed the proper safety procedures and did not harm anyone. As you read the chapters on the different types of guns, ammunition and techniques, think about the safety procedures and their applications. If, for whatever reasons, you do not understand the applications, read this chapter again and, if necessary, many times. It's a short chapter but failing to follow the safety procedures outlined in it could shorten someone's life.

LOADING AND UNLOADING

The muzzle of the gun must always be kept in a safe direction. This includes taking into consideration all the reasons for safety as outlined in this chapter. **While loading you always keep your trigger finger out of the trigger guard.** This finger should be touching the outside of the trigger guard or the frame. Remember, your finger should only be on the trigger when you intend to fire or dry fire or to release the hammer into the down position. Before loading your ammunition each round should be inspected. Check for any abnormalities such as a bulging of the casing, a protruding primer, or any other visible abnormalities which could cause a misfire or be a safety hazard.

Loading the revolver (double action only)

The cylinder release is pushed. You grasp the barrel of the gun with the weak hand and let the cylinder drop open. Your thumb, index and little finger will hold the weapon, and your middle and ring fingers will be placed through the frame, resting on the cylinder and holding it firmly open. With your strong hand insert the cartridges one at a time. Be sure that they are completely seated in position, and then gently close the cylinder and rotate it until you hear it click into place.

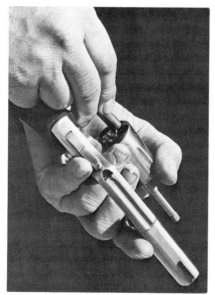

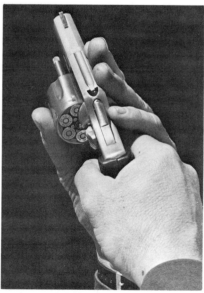

Insert the cartridges "one at a time" until the cylinder is fully loaded. Note how cylinder is held firmly by fingers.

Re-grip and gently close the cylinder and rotate it until it clicks into place. Note position of fingers.

Unloading the double action revolver

Keep the hammer in the down position and the revolver pointed in a safe direction with your finger out of the trigger guard. Grasp the gun exactly as you would to load it. Position the gun so that the barrel is pointing up and press the ejector rod all the way down. All the cartridges should fall out, however, always check to make sure that all the cartridges are ejected. Always check the entire cylinder itself, each hole individually, to make sure it is empty. Then close the cylinder, gently rotating it until it clicks back into place.

Push cylinder release and position fingers in preparation for opening.

Push open cylinder, hold it firmly and place thumb on ejector rod.

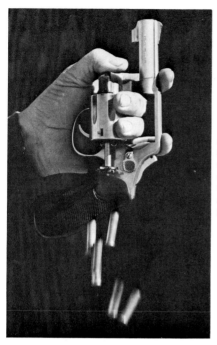

Turn the muzzle "straight up" and then the thumb briskly pushes ejector rod to its bottom position and all spent cases are "ejected." Be sure not to move your arm in a throwing motion. This will impede the ejection process. Also, be certain to check each chamber to be sure none of the cases have somehow stayed in place.

Loading the Semi-automatic Pistol

Use your strong hand to firmly grasp the pistol using the correct grip. Insert the loaded magazine with the weak hand. Then grasp the slide serrations, located on the rear of the slide, pull the slide back all the way. Remember to keep your trigger finger out of the trigger guard. If you have problems pulling the slide back, cocking the hammer will make the slide move back easier. Firmly guide the slide back into place so the weapon can chamber the first round. Don't let it slam shut or do it too slowly or it could jam. When you initially insert the magazine you should feel and hear it click into place. If the magazine isn't properly seated, it will not feed the ammunition. Make sure you "click" the magazine into place! You are still not fully loaded as you now have a magazine with one less round in it than its capacity. To load the pistol to full capacity, put the safety in the "on" position and then remove the magazine. Either holster your pistol or put it down safely on a table. **Always be muzzle conscious!** Take another round and refill the magazine and then place the now full magazine back into the pistol. Always keep in mind, when doing this, that you have a live round already chambered in the pistol and proceed with proper caution. Your pistol is now fully loaded with a round in the chamber and a full magazine. **Do not** buy extension magazines. The semi-automatic is engineered by the manufacturer to hold a certain number of rounds which are fed in a precise angle under a precise tension. Most of these extension magazines are not made by the original manufacturer and are too unreliable to depend on for self defense.

Note:
The loading and unloading sequences for the semi-auto pistol are for the Colt Government series. Other pistols have variations from these procedures. Always refer to your manufacturer's owner's manual.

Pistol is held firmly in strong hand; trigger finger is straight alongside of frame. Not in trigger guard or any part of the trigger. *Fully loaded magazine is inserted.*

Loaded magazine is in place and as upward pressure is applied with palm of weak hand to magazine base, an audible click should be heard when it is fully seated Note: Magazine in this photo has a rubber base pad installed. These are easily added to your magazine bases and are an aid to positive seating.

Proper position of trigger finger during all loading and unloading procedures. This is an absolute must!!

Grasp slide with weak hand as shown using serrations for slip free grip.

Pull slide back to end of its travel. Gently but firmly move slide forward until round is chambered and slide is fully closed.

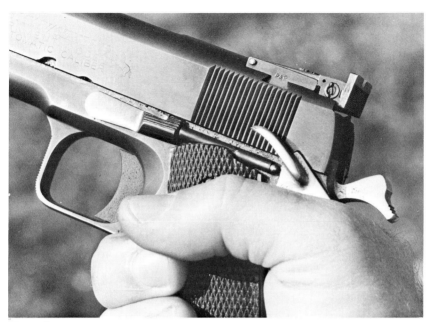

The safety is immediately put to the "on" position with thumb of strong hand. Magazine should now be removed and another round inserted. Fully loaded magazine is reinserted. You now have a fully loaded pistol. Magazine release button should be operated with thumb of the strong hand. This may require a slight grip adjustment of the strong hand so your thumb can comfortably reach the release button. This grip adjustment is used only when changing or removing magazines.

Unloading the Semi-automatics

Place the safety in the "on" position and keep your finger out of the trigger guard. Press the magazine release button as you are firmly grasping the pistol with your strong hand. Grasp the magazine with your weak hand and remove it. **You still have a round in the chamber which must be removed.** Novices make the mistake of thinking the gun is unloaded completely when the magazine is removed. **It is not!** Always be muzzle conscious and keep the gun pointed in a safe position. You must now put the safety in the "off" position on most semi-automatics, or you won't be able to pull the slide back. Turn the pistol upside down and pull the slide back with your weak hand until you feel the remaining round fall into your hand. Put the round in your pocket or some other safe place where you won't forget about it. Turn the gun right side up and pull the slide back again to visually inspect the chamber. Point the gun in a safe direction and drop the hammer by pulling the trigger. The pistol is now unloaded and can be safely stored since there is no magazine in the gun, the chamber is empty, and the hammer is in the down position.

The first step in unloading the auto-pistol is to remove the magazine.

While keeping the muzzle in a safe direction and your fingers away from the trigger, disengage the safety (if applicable). Turn the pistol upside down. Cup your weak hand over the ejection port and open the slide fully. The chambered round should come out in your hand.

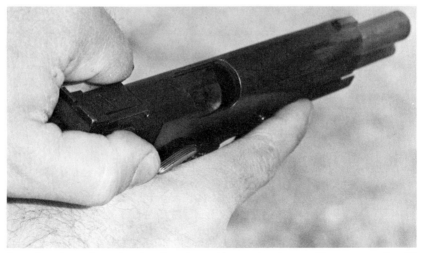

Even though you have the chambered round in your hand, you still must open the slide and visually inspect the chamber. This is the only way to be absolutely sure the gun is empty.

Point the pistol in a safe direction, press the trigger and allow the hammer to drop. Note! Some auto-pistols can be damaged by this process; check your owner's manual or with a gunsmith to be certain you won't harm your weapon.

SOME COMMON PROBLEMS

Revolver

If you can't get the rounds in the cylinder, you probably have the wrong ammunition. Every gun, including pistols, are marked as to what ammunition can be used in it. A common mistake is thinking that because a .357 Magnum can take .38 Special ammunition, that the same is true in reverse. It isn't. If one bullet doesn't seat properly in the cylinder, you probably have a dirty chamber. A high primer could prevent you from closing the cylinder or from being able to rotate it once it is closed.

Another common problem would be light firing pin hits. In this situation your firing pin will strike the primer, but not with enough force to ignite the powder. This problem is generally caused by an improperly modified double action trigger mechanism which has been lightened too much. This could also be caused by ammunition in which the primer is not seated to its full depth. With magnum loadings another problem could be caused by bullets which are not properly crimped. The heavy recoil of these loads can cause bullets to move forward in the case preventing the cylinder from rotating. The only way to clear this is to remove the offending round.

Semi-Automatic

Two of the most common problems are when a round gets "hung up" or you have what is known as a "stove pipe." When a round gets "hung up," this means it doesn't go fully into the chamber. When this happens you should lock the slide back with the slide stop and remove the magazine. Then turn the gun upside down, making sure the gun is pointed in a safe direction, and remove the round our rounds which are not chambering properly. A "stove pipe" occurs when an ejecting empty case is caught between the hood of the barrel and the breech face. The case mouth will point up or perpendicular to the barrel preventing it from chambering the next round out of the magazine. It is commonly caused by a round with a weak powder charge, or if it is a constant problem, by too heavy a recoil spring. To clear this jam the weak hand little finger is swept back across the top of the slide and ejection port, catching the stuck case and flipping it back in a rearward snapping motion. By doing it this way, the gun will automatically finish chambering the next round, and you are ready to continue firing.

Another problem is when the slide on the auto does not fully close. This can be caused by a dirty gun, or by a round which has a slightly oversized case. This can usually be remedied instantly by pushing with both thumbs on the back of the slide until it is fully closed. Once again the handgun is ready to fire once this procedure has been completed. However, when performing any of the aforementioned procedures, it is of absolute importance that all fingers be kept away from the trigger. Your out of action time while correcting the "stove pipe" or when the slide does not fully close will be minimal. If you have a round which is "hung up," obviously it will take time to clear the gun, reinsert your magazine, and chamber a fresh round. The more you practice, the quicker you will become at solving these problems.

There is one problem which both the revolver and semi-automatic share. At some time when firing you may hear a very faint pop, noticeably softer than your regular shots. This could signal a round which had a primer but no powder. The primer only has enough force to drive the bullet an inch or two in the barrel. When practicing, you should stop firing immediately, clear the handgun, and examine the barrel. If a bullet is stuck, it is usually driven out with light tapping using cleaning rod or wood dowel that fits easily inside the barrel. Under no circumstances should you fire a live round to remove a stuck bullet.

One last thing the revolvers and semi-automatics have in common is that if any problem persists have a **qualified gunsmith repair it for you!**

It takes a number of components to develop correct form.

CHAPTER 5

BASIC SHOOTING STYLES AND TECHNIQUES

In all sports and academic pursuits the experts often disagree on what techniques and styles should be taught and implemented. The styles and techniques we teach have been developed and proven successful in our ISI self defense training classes and are also being used by many police departments throughout the United States. We feel confident they will provide you with a quick, easily adaptable, accurate method to learn how to properly fire the handgun. There are variations but, in our opinion, these techniques are the best for you to use. As you read this chapter you might find yourself getting confused; after all, this is probably new to most of you. Many of you will find that following the instructions with your handgun, step by step, as described and illustrated, that it will come quite quickly to you. Like all things that are new to us, you might find the grip and stances awkward at first, but after practicing them you will find these techniques do exactly what we say. They provide you with a consistent, accurate method of shooting, giving you maximum control and speed.

GRIP

When holding the revolver, the strong hand (your strong hand is determined by the hand you feel you are the most dexterous with) is placed as high as possible on the grip without interfering with the movement of the hammer. The back of the grip will fit firmly in the web of your hand between the index finger and thumb. As a guide take your index finger and place it on the trigger so the beginning of the second joint is centered on the trigger. The position of the strong hand should now come naturally as your hand wraps around the grip with your thumb coming to rest above the middle finger of your strong hand. Now, with your weak hand, place the index finger over the middle finger of your strong hand. Your weak hand index finger should be roughly centered over the strong hand middle finger and overlap onto the strong side of the gun. This will vary according to your hand size. The middle, ring and little fingers of your weak hand should now fall into place over the fingers of the strong hand. The last, and the most common mistake, is the placement of the weak hand thumb. It should be placed above the thumb of the strong hand on the **weak side** of the handgun. Do not wrap your weak hand thumb around the back of the grip toward the strong hand side of the gun! You won't have the proper control if you do and you could also interfere with the action of the hammer. If you develop the habit of putting the weak hand thumb in the wrong position you will also have a problem with the slide on the auto pistol. If you keep your grip consistent, as described, you will be able to shoot both the semi-automatic and the double action revolver with basically the same grip.

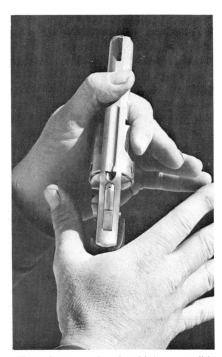

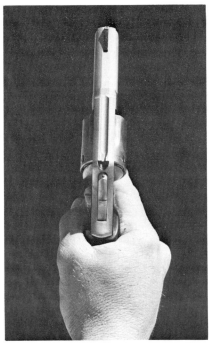

Place the strong hand as high as possible on the grip without interfering with the hammer movement.

Using your trigger finger as a guide, position the rest of the fingers on the grip.

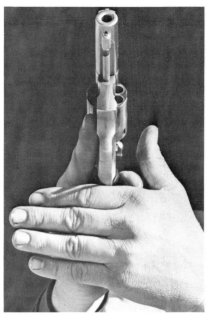

Place the weak hand touching the base of the trigger guard.

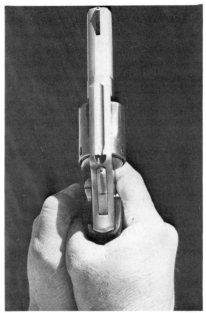

Position the rest of the weak hand fingers against the other hand. (Note: How thumbs lock together)

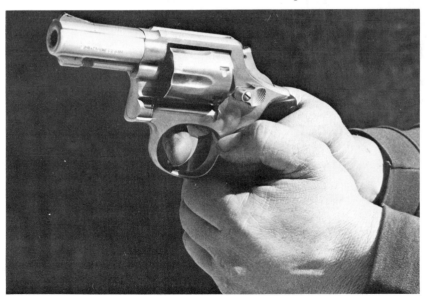

This is the proper revolver grip. Take special notice of the position of the trigger finger. Both hands should feel comfortably interlocked, and the heels of both hands should have contact.

The grip on the semi-automatic pistol has only one basic difference and that is the position of your strong hand index finger on the trigger. This gun does not require as much strength to pull the trigger as the revolver. You can gain maximum trigger control by placing the pad of your index finger (first joint) in a centered position on the trigger. The rest of the gripping position is basically the same. One word of caution, you must be careful not to grip the semi-automatic pistol so high up on the grip that it interferes with the slide action. If you do, your hand may be severely cut by the action of the slide as it ejects and rechambers a round when the gun is fired.

The basic hold we recommend is a two fisted grip. This provides you with maximum control. You must push with the strong arm and pull back with equal pressure with the weak arm. This will exert equal pressure from both hands on the weapon. This is an isometric type of hold and you want to use as much pressure as possible without "setting up" muscle tremors from squeezing too hard. This procedure is essential and insures proper control of a powerful handgun. Also, gripping the gun as high as possible without interfering with the hammer on the revolver or the slide action on the auto pistol will allow you more control over the recoil. Recoil is simple physics. When the bullet exits the barrel, the gun will react to the force of the expulsion in the opposite direction. By gripping your hands as close as possible to the line of force of the bullet's exit, you will have maximum control over the recoil. This will enable you to quickly recover for accurate shooting when rapid firing both the pistol and the revolver. For those with average or large hands we have found an advantage to positioning the weak hand index finger around the trigger guard. This positioning of the weak hand index finger offers added leverage in controlling recoil. If your hands are large enough you should try firing your auto pistol this way. When using this hold you must have the trigger guard checkered, otherwise your finger would slip off and thus nullify the advantage you gained with this hold.

Note! Double action semi-automatic pistols will require the trigger finger to be placed on the first joint of the trigger finger because of the heavy pull (very similar to revolver).

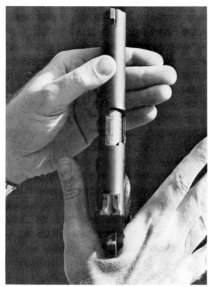

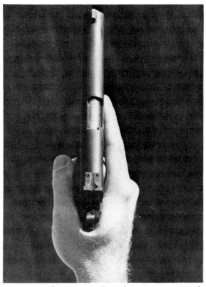

Grasp pistol with strong hand. Note web of hand is high on grip safety tang, but has enough clearance to let the slide function without interference.

Fingers of strong hand are wrapped around grip.

View showing recommended position of strong hand thumb. Strong hand thumb is used to operate the safety lever and magazine release on the Colt Government model auto.

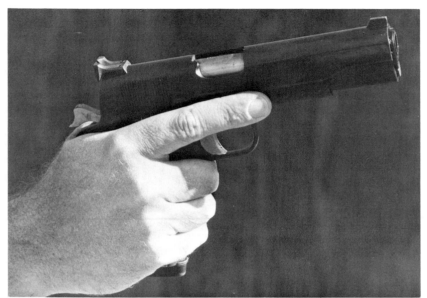

Note: Trigger finger is straight alongside frame rail, never in trigger guard or on the trigger until actually ready to fire.

Another view of correct grip.

Weak hand fingers wrap around strong hand fingers. Note position of trigger finger. Pad of first joint is centered on trigger. Shooter is now ready to fire pistol.

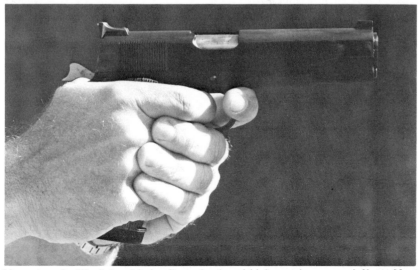

Alternate grip. Weak hand index finger is placed high on trigger guard. Note: Most effective when trigger guard is checkered.

THE BASIC STANCE

When shooting from the standing position the **WEAVER** stance must be utilized. This method was developed by a San Diego County Sheriff Deputy, Jack Weaver, and is widely used. It has proven to be more effective than earlier shooting stances. The Weaver stance consists of standing with your feet approximately shoulder width apart at about a 45° angle to the target. The right handed shooter should have his left foot in the forward position and should be leaning slightly forward with approximately sixty percent of his weight on the balls of his feet. The knees are slightly bent and the leg muscles should naturally feel flexed if you have assumed the proper position and weight distribution. The elbow of the left arm is raised at a 45° angle and is bent considerably more than the right arm. Both wrists are locked solidly so that if someone were to come up to you and try to force the gun upwards there would be a great deal of resistance. Your upper body and arms may move but your wrists should remain level with the barrel of the gun and should not flex. This not only allows you to absorb the recoil better but will also allow you to resight your follow up shots more quickly and result in more accuracy.

When you shoot there is always the question of whether or not to use both eyes and, if you only use one eye, which one? The problem most people have when shooting with both eyes is that they see a double image. If you have this problem, and more than likely you will, you will have to squint one eye. If you are one of the rare people who can use both eyes you will have a slight advantage because your field of vision will be wider. If you can use only one eye you must determine which eye is your master eye. Generally you will feel one or the other eye is the one you see with best. If both eyes seem equal, we have found that most people feel comfortable using the eye on the side of the strong hand.

Basic Weaver stance for automatic or revolver.

View of stance. Note position of feet. They should be at 45-degree angle to firing line. Your body should be leaning slightly forward.

Position of upper body using Weaver stance. Head is slightly bent to the right to clearly see sights. Properly applied this technique makes your body into a very solid gun mount.

Side view of upper body position using Weaver stance. Right arm is slightly bent; left arm is bent at 45-degree angle. Right arm is slightly pushing out, while left arm is slightly pulling back. Wrists are solidly locked.

When training for self defense with the handgun you could say you are training as if the target is your enemy. Obviously this is how we feel you should train. There are other positions you will have to practice besides standing, but we feel that there is a right way and a wrong way to first learn how to do anything. When you are first learning the Weaver stance, our described grip and general basics, will allow you to quickly become an accurate shooter. Once you are familiar with the basic stance and grip you can then move on to the other techniques and styles of shooting. Should you have to defend yourself you may find that you have to shoot from behind a couch, underneath a table or from any number of positions, but you will have the confidence to handle the situation because you have a thorough knowledge of the basics. We want to make it clear that you must have a thorough understanding of the fundamentals of accurate shooting before you will gain anything from practicing some of the other positions.

FUNDAMENTALS OF MARKSMANSHIP

There are a few basic ingredients to marksmanship. The first is your **sight picture.** The proper sight picture means that once you see your target your focus is brought to your front sight, you will actually be focusing on your front sight. What you should see is a razor sharp front sight and the rear sight will be slightly blurred as will be the target. Revolvers and pistols generally have a rear sight which has a squared off notch. When looking into your rear sight towards the front sight it should be lined up so that there is an equal amount of light showing on either side of the front sight. The top of the front sight should be flush with an imaginary line across the top of the rear sight.

The perfect sight picture. During your practice sessions, always strive to maintain your focus on the front sight. This will help keep your shots in the narrowest "cone of fire."

Target in focus.

Rear sight in focus.

Front sight high.

Front sight low.

Front sight, left.

Front sight, right.

Front sight low, right.

Front sight high, left.

The second ingredient is what is known as **hold.** Once you have achieved the proper sight picture you should practice holding this picture on the target you wish to hit. If you have a good sight picture but don't hold it steady you are sure to miss your target. A common complaint is that people find that they shake slightly and can't hold their sight picture. This is usually caused from gripping too tightly which causes your muscles to tense up resulting in a slight tremor. Relax your grip only enough to stop the tremors.

The third important ingredient is the **trigger squeeze or trigger control.** The trigger must be squeezed back in a straight smooth motion with your finger. At the same time you must maintain the proper sight picture. The sight picture and the trigger pull are the two most important ingredients of accurate shooting. Their development and practice are critical in building your skill.

Everyone who wants to shoot well will have to "dry fire." Dry firing is a method of practicing with an unloaded handgun. It is important that you do this exercise with the same determination and level of concentration as you do at the range with your loaded handgun. You should use a dry firing target about four to five feet high off the ground and assume the Weaver stance and get the proper sight picture. Once you have the sight picture smoothly pull the trigger until the hammer falls. When dry firing you should practice to the point at which you can maintain that sight picture for several seconds after the hammer falls. It is not only excellent practice for the beginner but also a good way to maintain your skill in between practice sessions at the target range. Keep your dry firing sessions short, about five to eight minutes, three to five times a day, or your concentration will diminish and your muscles will become tense.

We want to stress the importance of safety once again when dry firing. Negligent dry fire can be as deadly as negligent live fire. Never point your firearm at anything you are unwilling to destroy. Never place dry firing targets, or use as a target, a surface which cannot fully absorb a round fired accidentally. A round penetrating that surface could injure someone on the other side. Never place dry fire targets, or use as a target, a surface which could cause an accidentally fired round to ricochet. Some handguns are not suitable for dry fire, and will be damaged by it. Check with the manufacturer or a local gunsmith. Observe all safety guidelines when dry firing.

When you practice with a loaded handgun you will have to contend with recoil. It is very important to master the fourth ingredient of accurate shooting known as **"follow through."** What you will try to do is to hold the sight picture through the recoil. This is actually impossible, but by trying to do this you will find that you will quickly regain your sight picture and will be able to fire rapid accurate shots. This will also help you to avoid flinching from anticipation of the recoil.

While rapid firing you must be aware of the necessity of fully releasing the trigger after each shot. If you don't fully release the trigger, the trigger mechanism will not be able to reset for the next shot.

We can not stress enough the importance of holding the focus on the front sight and having a smooth, steady trigger pull. **The trigger pull can easily ruin any shot.** There is little margin for error. If you jerk the trigger or anticipate the shot going off and flinch, have an irregular grip or don't concentrate on the concept of follow through, your shot will not hit its intended spot on the target or miss entirely. Missing your target is never the gun's fault. If the sight picture isn't held until the bullet leaves the barrel, the bullet will not go where you want. The bullet travels exactly where the barrel is pointed when the bullet exits. During your dry firing exercise try placing a coin on the front sight of your handgun (you can balance a coin on most front sights although a few don't lend themselves to this exercise) and practice smoothly pulling the trigger while maintaining the sight picture. If you jerk the trigger or flinch, the coin will fall off.

The International Shootists Inc. Home-Practice Dry Firing Kit is designed to aid shooters in developing proper technique. It includes instructions, various "dry-firing" targets and a chart for simulating distances.

Assuming that you have become proficient with your Weaver stance you are now ready to learn the techniques and styles necessary to coordinate speed and accuracy as well as learning how to shoot from different positions. When we speak of speed we are talking about two aspects. First, the ability to fire multiple shots accurately and rapidly and second, how to quickly bring your weapon into use whether drawing from a holster or just bringing it from a rested ready position.

AIM FIRING is the first method of shooting that develops your skills in both speed and accuracy. In some self defense situations you will not be able to stand in your Weaver stance, focused on your target, mainly because you may not have the time needed. Your attacker may not allow you to see him first and give you that extra split second to get a perfect sight picture. But, from becoming proficient in this method you will find you have developed the basics necessary to be an accurate shot using other methods. In AIM FIRING you first assume the Weaver stance as previously described. You will use the two handed grip with your trigger finger outside the trigger guard. (Not on the trigger! Especially important with auto pistols. Your finger should just be resting against the frame above the trigger guard). The safety should be engaged with your thumb positioned ready for instant release. Once you have identified the target bring the gun to eye level while thrusting it towards the target. Your eyes should be on the target and your hands should be pushed to where your eyes are looking. You will find that your hands will naturally go to where your eyes are focusing. Do not "cowboy" the gun. This term refers to those who raise the gun above eye level and then bring the gun back down to eye level. This blocks your vision and wastes valuable time. Now that you are in position, you want to locate the front sight on the portion of the target you wish to hit. As soon as this is accomplished you will then focus 100% on the front sight to get a perfect sight picture. Hold the sight picture and smoothly and quickly pull the trigger. This is the most reliable and effective way to shoot. **AIM FIRING** means that you are aiming at your target by focusing on the front sight. This method will enable you to keep your shots in the narrowest cone of fire. When you practice start off slow and increase your pace little by little. At first your muscles may be sore but the more you practice the easier it will get and the better shot you will become. If you are practicing properly your shots shouldn't wander off the target. If they do, slow down, go over the fundamentals again before you develop bad habits. Without absolute adherence and practice on your part it is unlikely that you will ever develop into a competent shooter. This method is the foundation you will use to build all your skills upon. We all know that without a solid foundation nothing substantial can be built. **AIM FIRING** is an absolute necessity to master.

POINT SHOOTING is very valuable in low light situations where the front sight and target are difficult to see. What this really does is allow your weapon to become an extension of your arms. This method is slightly faster than Aim firing but not as accurate. The weapon is brought to eye level with the same motions used in aim firing but the difference is that instead of focusing on your front sight your eyes will look at the spot on the target that you wish to hit over the barrel or the slide of your gun. At best you can be fairly accurate up to a distance of about thirty feet. When practicing this method you will find it difficult to be accurate when shooting at the head portion of a silhouette target. After practicing you should be fairly accurate within a twenty foot range when firing at the chest area of a silhouette target. Obviously we feel you are in a stronger position in a self defense situation if you can Aim fire but, if the light doesn't permit or time is of the essence, **POINT SHOOTING** is the next best method.

INSTINCT SHOOTING could also be called unsighted fire and is known as "hip shooting." It has limited usefulness but, in some cases, it can be a very valuable skill to know. Therefore, you should take time to learn and practice it. The reliability range is only about three to five feet but, in a close range situation, you may have no choice but to utilize this method of shooting. It provides the absolute maximum speed in getting off the first shot and is very useful in a tight situation where extending your arms would put you in jeopardy of having your firearm taken away from you.

You will be using only one hand to hold your weapon, usually your strong hand, unsupported and your elbow will be bent about 90% to the ground with your forearm tucked against your side. We recommend the elbow being slightly behind your back with your wrist locked and your forearm parallel to the ground. Your weapon will be fired as soon as your forearm and the barrel of the gun are parallel to the ground. You will still need to squeeze the trigger straight back in a quick but smooth motion.

The obvious disadvantage of instinct shooting is that at ranges of more than three to five feet it is totally unreliable. Even within this range you will have to practice to become proficient in its use. If your target is beyond the three to five foot range you should have the extra tenth of a second more than you need to get the gun into one of the other positions using the two handed grip and the Weaver stance.

When you practice all three of these shooting styles you will realize three things; first, why instinct shooting is only advisable when you don't have the time or space to use a more reliable method, second, why we recommend practicing all three shooting styles and third, the reliability and accuracy of all three methods.

There is always the possibility that you might have to shoot with one hand. One of your hands could be disabled or you might need to use one hand to hold a flashlight, to telephone the police, or any number of other reasons. If at all possible it is better to shoot with your strong hand. Your basic grip and stance will be the same. The same principles for accurate two handed shooting will still apply. You will still want to try and pull the trigger straight back in a smooth manner. If you can bring your weak hand into a supporting position, that would be preferable. If you can't, try to keep the weak or disabled hand close to the abdomen or chest area to help you achieve a better balance.

Hopefully you will never have to shoot with the weak hand, but you might not have any choice. The method is the same as for the strong hand shooting. It is always possible that your strong hand could be disabled but, by practicing weak hand shooting, knowing you have the ability to shoot accurately with your weak hand will be comforting and possibly life saving.

Both the strong hand and weak hand shooting skills should be worked on regularly when you practice. We feel, although you will probably spend only a limited amount of your practice time on these exercises, it is valuable and necessary.

This is an example of "cowboying the gun." Do not let yourself fall into this very bad habit. You temporarily block your vision and waste valuable time.

When practicing "weak" (top) or "strong" (bottom) handed shooting, tuck the loose arm in tight to your body for balance. If one of your arms is disabled, it can possibly be used in some manner for support in a self-defense situation. Notice how much less control you'll have when firing with one hand, but realize it is something you can learn to do well.

85

Now that you understand the basic techniques of markmanship we have to take another step into the basics of self defense shooting. This involves shooting from cover and concealment. As we have stated in our tactics chapter, cover is considered any object that will protect you from the destructive force of a bullet and concealment only enables you to be in an undetectable or hidden position. In most cases you will be firing from concealment as there are very few objects in your home which will provide cover. However, both are similar in the support they provide and the following basic techniques apply to both cover and concealment.

BRACE SHOOTING, when time allows, has many advantages. If you have any time at all you should be able to use this method. Brace shooting is also known as SUPPORT SHOOTING and there are several different variations of this method. It is to your advantage to utilize the most appropriate form of BRACE SHOOTING whenever possible in conjunction with cover or concealment.

The first we will discuss is the basic corner wall or barricade technique. There are two ways of utilizing this method. One is using the weak or strong hand against a wall surface. The back of the hand is placed against the wall and used for supporting the position of your gun. The other variation is using the knuckles of the weak hand against the wall surface. This can be more difficult to learn than the back of the hand method but does allow you to protect yourself better because you will expose less of your body during a confrontation.

We recommend you practice both ways and find the one that best suits your body build and strength. The caliber of your handgun and its recoil could also be a deciding factor. When practicing you should use a glove on the hand that is against the wall to prevent bruising or abrasions.

Shooting from behind "cover" or "concealment" is a very important part of your training.

This is the position of feet when shooting from behind cover or concealment. Feet are parallel to wall about shoulder width apart. The distance you stand from the wall will be determined by the length of your arms. You should be leaning slightly forward into the wall used for support. When this position is correctly used, only a small part of your head and part of your arm will be exposed.

This is all someone in front of your cover will see of you. Not only are the chances of you being hit much less, you are shooting from a steadier position than "off hand."

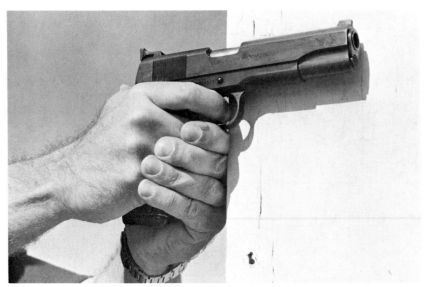

Right side knuckle technique (for right-handed shooter). Use your regular two-handed grip. Place the knuckles of the weak hand against the wall as shown. Lean your body weight slightly into your weak hand knuckles for support.

Left side knuckle technique (for right-handed shooter). Pistol is canted (angled). Knuckles of the left hand are against the wall. Use regular grip. Cant (angle) pistol as shown.

This is an illustration only to show the position of weak hand on wall. Do not assume this position in this manner. Both your hands should be on the gun before you make contact with the wall.

Note: You should have at least ¼" clearance between the gun and the wall. If this clearance is not maintained, the slide (autos) or cylinder (revolvers) would make contact with the wall and impede operation. This could cause the gun to malfunction.

Left side knuckle technique (for right-hand shooters). View showing position of trigger finger. Clearance must be maintained between wall and trigger finger. This is one determining factor in how much the pistol must be canted.

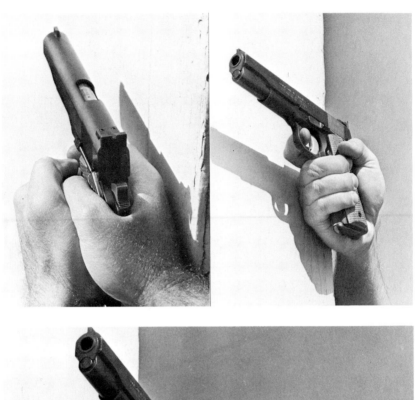

The back of hand barricade technique for left side use your regular two handed grip. Back of strong hand is used for support against wall.

The back of the hand barricade technique for right side. Use your regular two handed grip. Back of left hand is used for support against wall.

91

The ideal support technique would be to give support to both hands. Most any piece of furniture in your home will give you the support you need providing it has some weight and is solid enough to stay upright. A table, couch, cabinet, bed or other similar objects are good choices. Don't depend on a wobbly table or rocking chair or any object that would fall over or move easily from your body weight or slight movement. As a rule, this position can provide you with maximum concealment and provide a very effective, solid position from which to shoot. Preplanning is very important and you should decide before trouble happens exactly where you could conceal yourself and what would provide the best support for shooting. Once your fundamentals are sound this method will come quite easy with a minimum amount of practice time.

Shooting from the **PRONE** position is the most accurate and consistent position from which to fire a handgun. It does, however, take time to assume this position. With your body prone your elbows will be on the surface of the floor providing support to both hands. Your head will probably be slightly bent up as, more than likely, you will have to shoot up unless an assailant is also in the same position or below you. This position does have some important disadvantages in self defense shooting. It takes more time to get into proper position and your field of vision will be effected because of limited mobility and your cover and concealment may be limited. The most serious disadvantage is that someone could fire down at you and miss but the bullet could hit you. A bullet can hit a hard, flat surface and then travel parallel to that surface. These drawbacks make it a poor choice for defensive shooting.

Another position you might have to shoot from is the **KNEELING** position. You might have concealment which is not high enough for you to stand behind. If possible, place your weight on one knee, preferably the strong hand side with the weak side knee up. This position will give you the best balance for absorbing recoil. Your legs should be spread further apart than they would be standing. If you don't have a solid object to use as a brace you can put your weak side elbow on the knee that is up. You should always have one knee up rather than both knees on the ground. You will have better balance and the extra mobility needed should you have to move quickly. This can be a very useful position when shooting from concealment or cover.

NIGHT SHOOTING

When you shoot in any low light situation there are several potential problems which you must be able to handle. First, it is a good idea to have a flat white paint of some type applied to your front sight. This would give you at least a chance at aim firing if the room is not too dark. With the flat white, if you can see your target you will be able to use aim

The kneeling position is very adaptable to many self defense situations. Practicing it should become part of your regular shooting exercises. Notice how the "weak arm" is supported by the left leg.

(Left) The proper "rested ready" position. The handgun is held in your normal grip with muzzle near parallel to the ground. Trigger finger is positioned inside trigger guard but not touching trigger and the safety is engaged with thumb ready for instant release (autos). (Right) In one smooth motion the gun is thrust towards the target and the shooter is instantly ready for action.

fire. If you do not have flat white on your sight, or the room is too dark you will have to point fire. Whenever you can use your sights do so! Remember also, when you can't be absolutely positive of your target don't shoot!

Another area of preparation both mentally and from the standpoint of practice is the muzzle flash. It will distract you, and after firing your first shots, it could effect your vision for several minutes. You should fire two quick shots. With practice the development of muscle memory will be helpful in enabling you to get back on target should you need to fire additional shots.

You can adapt daytime practice which will help prepare you for night shooting. First, point shooting is very important to practice. Second, we mentioned muscle memory. With your weapon in the rested ready position, focus on a target, then close both eyes and bring the gun to where you think the proper sight alignment on that target would be. When you open your strong eye, you will see how close you are, and in what way it is off. After practicing this, you will find that you can get extremely close if not right on the mark through the concept of building your muscle memory. This exercise will be helpful as well in other areas of your shooting marksmanship. By practicing this in your Weaver stance even in very dark conditions you are likely to hit dead center. Also, because of the need to use a flashlight you must practice your strong hand shooting skills. It is highly recommended that you spend time practicing with a flashlight in your weak hand. You should also keep in mind that just because you will not be able to align the sights in a low light situation as you could under normal light conditions, does not mean you can be lax in concentrating on a smooth trigger pull. It is more important in night shooting to be especially smooth. More than likely you will already be a little off center, and you don't need to compound the problem by being careless.

If you have access to an outdoor range where night shooting is possible you should practice at night. It will build up your confidence in that if you practice what we preach, you will find you can be very accurate, also, you will know what to expect from muzzle flash.

SHOOTING MULTIPLE TARGETS

The proper technique in firing on multiple targets is to make your body like a gun mount, in which you will pivot wasting no time or motion. Your arm swing and upper body motion should be locked. Within a 180 degree range your feet should remain stationary. Your arms should remain in the same relationship to your chest, as should your wrists in relation to your eyes and forearms. This will make your body like a gun mount, turning as if your waistline is the bearing on which the gun mount turns. This will keep you from swinging your arms and thus wasting time from having to realign your hand-eye relationship.

The tendency for new shooters is to overswing a target which they move to engage. This occurs sometimes when firm enough body control is not exerted by the shooter. Once the shooter is moving properly from target to target, he must then be sure to "lock" on the target. "Lock" means to be sure that the movement has stopped before the shot is fired. This requires a conscious effort by the shooter to know that he has fully stopped on target. During practice it is easy to tell if you are "overswinging" because your shots will be grouped towards the direction of your swing. In order to correct this, make sure you are coming to a full stop before you actuate the trigger. This takes practice, and as with all techniques, increase your speed gradually; in time you will master this important technique.

All the basic shooting styles and techniques we have discussed might be needed at sometime and therefore should be practiced. If, when practicing these different positions, you find that you are having problems shooting accurately it is probably due to your basic sighting and trigger pull fundamentals. **Always remember to concentrate on those basics.** You should be able to learn to shoot accurately from all the positions we described with proper adherence to our instructions and the necessary practice time.

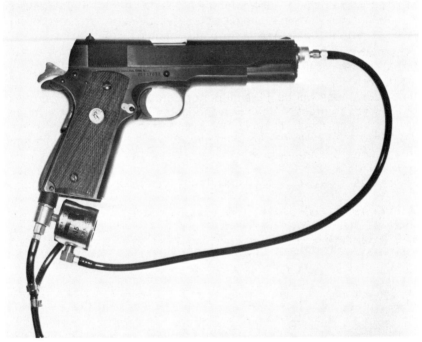

Firing Simulator for .45 Automatics. It is available from Advanced .45 Technology. This PNEUMATIC device actually cycles the slide, cocks the hammer and recoils as fast as the user can pull the trigger. Your gun can be converted in seconds to practice the fundamentals of accurate shooting at home. Especially good training aid for learning "follow-through."

RANGE PRACTICE

Actual live fire practice on a regular basis is a necessary part of your defensive training. You can not expect to become competent without work and we recommend practicing at least once a week at a target range. We have found that you can retain much more of your acquired abilities and skills when you go at least once a week and fire about fifty rounds. Some people try to make it a once a month affair where they shoot hundreds of rounds. The idea that any practice is better than no practice is only partially true. These once a monthers who "overshoot," as a rule, develop bad habits. You should never shoot beyond your ability to concentrate. As a rule, one hundred rounds in a day is the maximum most people can handle when properly concentrating. Beyond that, the shooter is shooting tired, his fundamentals become lax and even the best shooters will find their skills regress.

There are two basic types of ranges to choose from. If you are lucky, both will be available in your area. If not, most likely, you will find at least an indoor range in suburban areas, or outdoor ranges with restrictions. The disadvantage will be if the indoor or outdoor range near you does not allow you to practice defensive shooting. Many will not allow you to draw from a holster or to rapid fire. Even if you have a long drive we strongly suggest, at least once a month, you go to a range where you can practice your defensive shooting skills. Another possibility you may have is a local competition club which has the facilities to practice defensive shooting. An IPSC club is the best one to look for and to join. If none of these ranges are available and you decide to drive out into the country and make your own practice range, please keep several things in mind. First, make sure that you have a bullet-proof backstop such as a large hillside. Common sense tells you to stay away from populated areas and heavily travelled roads. Be sure to find out from your local authorities exactly where they will allow you to shoot.

When you go to a range, carry an equipment bag with you. This bag should contain hearing protection, either ear muffs or the soft foam inserts that can be washed and re-used, eye protection and any other shooting necessities. Ammunition and a surplus GI ammunition can is excellent for carrying for this purpose as it is steel and very durable as well as reasonably priced. A log book containing your notes from previous visits to check on your progress, bullseye and IPSC silhouette targets and target tape for patching holes in the targets.

Once you are at the range, we recommend that you do certain exercises. The first exercise is focusing on your front sight and smoothly squeezing the trigger. Use this exercise with your target by drawing a three inch circle on it and warm up by firing at the circle at a range of about seven yards. This will help you to get used to acquiring your front sight picture quickly. This exercise should be done from either the holster position if you plan on carrying your weapon or by holding the gun in the rested ready position. Another exercise is firing two shots into the center of the target as quickly as possible while still keeping them well centered. This should be done at about seven to ten yards. This exercise is very important because it will teach you to shoot as quickly as possible while still maintaining centered shots.

Another good exercise is engaging multiple targets at close range. Use three of your targets in staggered order: one five yards away, one seven yards and one ten yards away from you. As quickly as you can, try to hit each target once and then come back across the targets and fire at each one again. Then try shooting at a target from a barricaded position. You can use a chair if your range does not have actual barricades. Keep in mind that anytime you can shoot using concealment, you are better off defensively. Anyone who wants to learn to shoot well must practice dry firing, meaning that your weapon is unloaded. This will help you to learn to acquire a good sight picture and develop a smooth trigger pull. Many people flinch or jerk slightly while operating the trigger and this will cause the sight to move off target. To help overcome this tendency, while practicing dry firing, balance a coin on the front sight of the gun. If you are smoothly applying pressure on the trigger, the coin won't fall off.

You should practice all three styles of shooting during your range sessions; Aim, Point and Instinct shooting. Defensive shooting could require you to be in several different positions. It could also require that you fire your weapon from awkward positions or use only one hand, possibly your weak hand if your strong hand was injured. Take this into consideration when you are practicing. We suggest the following breakdown during each practice session.

Fifty percent standing position.

Thirty percent from behind cover and concealment.

Ten percent strong hand and ten percent weak hand using the standing and barricaded positions.

The following basic exercises will help you build a good foundation. You may not be able to do them all during each range visit depending on your development and time, but these will give you a goal to work toward. Understand that you are unlikely to be able to meet the time elements in the beginning, but as you become more adept, you should work toward successfully performing the exercises.

The "bullseye" target (left) and the IPSC "Milpark" silhouette (right) will be necessary to practice your defensive shooting skills. They are available from T.M. Industries.

A typical layout of targets for practicing your defensive shooting skills. We recommend the IPSC "Milpark" target shown because of the 10" circular vital zone. This is the area you should strive to keep all your shots located for maximum chance of stopping an assailant. This set up would allow you to practice the basic exercises (except bullseye).

99

Basic Exercises

25 yards — 6 shots — rested — "Bullseye" repeat once
25 yards — 6 shots — offhand — "Bullseye" (Offhand means standing, no artificial support.)
7 yards — 6 single draws — Freestyle — 1½ seconds
7 yards — 2 shots each on 3 targets — strong hand only — 5 seconds
7 yards — 2 shots each on 3 targets — weak hand only — 6 seconds
10 yards — 2 shots each on 3 targets, reload, 2 more shots on each — 10 seconds
10 yards — 1 shot — reload — 1 shot — 5 seconds, repeat 5 times
7 yards — 2 shots into target body — 1 shot to head 3 seconds — repeat 4 times

Students should decrease or increase time elements as proficiency dictates. (Times listed above are from a holstered position.)

Shooting from a concealed position should also be practiced if you are going to carry the handgun on your person at anytime for self defense reasons. You should also practice drawing from the position in which you keep your gun concealed whether it would be from a counter or from a shoulder holster or a purse. It will do you absolutely no good if you wear the gun in a shoulder holster and never practice drawing the gun from that position or if you can't grab your gun from a shelf under a counter in a quick, decisive manner.

When practicing, you should not continue if you become fatigued. Keep in mind that you should concentrate on every shot and that the maximum amount of rounds most people can shoot at one time is one hundred. At the point that you start to feel tired **STOP!** Pushing yourself to do more will result in your fundamentals becoming lax and bad habits developing.

Use your log book to keep a record of your performance. You will gain confidence by seeing the improvement you make as you practice. It will also detail the areas in which you are weak and show you where you need to spend more time practicing.

Many indoor ranges have limitations concerning the type of exercises you can do. Combat shooting exercises will probably not be available at these ranges. Also, you might not be able to rapid fire your handgun or practice your draw from concealment. What you can do is practice shooting the gun from a relaxed ready position. You really have no choice but to work within the limitations of the indoor range as they have rules they feel make it a safe place to practice for everyone. When at any range, whether indoors or outdoors, be aware of who is shooting around you, particularly on public ranges. You may see someone who is not following acceptable safety procedures. If, at anytime, someone is doing something you feel is not within the guidelines we outlined in our chapter on safety, ask the individual to stop that behavior. If they persist, complain to the range master and leave the premises.

The ammunition you will use for range practice will be separate from the ammunition you keep for self defense. Your range practice ammunition need not be what is known as full power. It isn't necessary nor is it desirable to use full power ammunition for practice. Full power ammunition causes undue wear on the equipment and also extra muzzle blast and recoil which can cause you to develop bad habits such as flinching. We're confident that in a self defense situation you will not notice the difference between the full power ammunition and the lighter load for practice.

If you have a problem during your practice, and even the most experienced shooters do, there are several things you can do to self correct the problem. First of all stop shooting. Ninety-nine percent of the time the problem isn't that the sights are off but that the shooter is anticipating the shot and jerking the trigger. To correct this, you should go back to your dry firing exercises until you are performing them properly. Most problems are caused by the shooter ignoring or forgetting to use the fundamentals. By stopping when you are not shooting the way you know you can, you will save yourself the problem of having to break bad habits. The other one percent of the time it could be your positioning, your grip or a variety of other minor problems that you can correct by going back over your basics and checking yourself.

RECREATION

Practicing your shooting skills doesn't have to be hard work. It can also be a great deal of fun. Many people find that once they begin to shoot, it is fun. There are probably gun clubs in your area which have local competition matches. These matches are both enjoyable and practical from the standpoint of further developing your skills.

The International Practical Shooting Confederation (IPSC) is an international sanctioning body for modern day Practical Pistol Competition. It sets the guidelines for these matches, both worldwide and local. The requirements are you must have a handgun of .38 caliber or larger, such as the .38 Special, 9mm semi-automatic, .45 ACP or other calibers. You have to use full power ammunition. Full power means it is up to the standards of factory produced ammunition and not light target loads. If you do join a gun club, try to find one that has been sanctioned by this group.

These matches will enable you to build your skills for self defense. They have little in common with the tactics utilized in real life confrontations but will help you build skills as far as making fast accurate shots as well as helping you learn to deal with stress from being under pressure. You will shoot from behind obstacles after moving from point to point. Your gun handling skills involved in drawing from a concealed position will be part of the competition. Combat silhouettes will be used and combat situations will be simulated. These competitions are fun and the firing courses are varied and they will round out your skills as an accomplished shooter.

In addition to your handgun, you will need some other equipment. You will need a secure, safe holster, extra speed loaders or magazines and factory equivalent ammunition.

To find out where a sanctioned gun club is located near you write to:

Jake Jatras
U.S. Regional Director
International Practical Shooting Confederation
P.O. Box 626
Sioux City, Iowa 51102-0626

We suggest that you observe a match and talk to the director. Most are very open to new shooters and the members, as a rule, are very friendly and helpful to new shooters, giving them tips on how to build their skills.

If, for some reason, a sanctioned club is not available in your area try to find a gun club that allows you some freedom in using the facilities. Also, try to get an idea of the type of competitions they have available. Some matches are really good for nothing more than fun and do little to build your skills. The Bullseye competitions are fine for practicing your basic skills but fall short in developing actual defensive shooting skills.

IPSC sanctioned matches specifically have not only provided a recreational method for building skills but have also made practical pistol shooting a rapidly growing sport. There is also a pro-circuit with money matches such as the Steel Challenge, (World Speed Shooting Championships), Bianchi Cup and Second Chance. This pro circuit has attracted, with its ever increasing purses, shooters from all over the world. Every two years IPSC directs a world championship match in which five man teams represent countries from all over the world. The boom has also taken place in local competitions and are set up in classifications so a shooter can compete on their own particular skill level. More and more women are joining these clubs and participating in matches as well.

CARRYING A CONCEALED HANDGUN

If you decide to carry a handgun on your person, it should always be fully loaded and ready for instant action. The modern double action revolver should be fully loaded with the hammer down, and the semi-automatic pistol should have a round in the chamber and a fully loaded magazine with the weapon's safety in the "on" position. **Never carry a revolver with the hammer cocked.** You should, of course, check all the applicable laws in your area and get any necessary permits required to allow you to carry a loaded firearm concealed.

There are different methods of carrying a concealed handgun, some better than others depending on the circumstances. For maximum concealability we recommend the Kidney Carry. In this carry the gun is positioned near the rear portion of the kidney (located in the small of your back). It should be positioned to the extreme right or left of this area on your strong hand side. It shouldn't be carried so far forward as to be visible on the side. The handgun will be carried with the barrel pointing down and slightly to the rear and the grip slightly forward. You should not keep the handgun simply tucked into your waistband because this doesn't provide a secure enough hold to keep the gun positioned correctly. The best way to carry it would be in a holster specifically designed to be placed inside the waistband of a pair of pants. This is a very light holster that snaps on to a belt. With a jacket or a shirt that doesn't have to be tucked in, you can wear a holster on the outside of your waistband and still enjoy maximum concealment as well as quick access to your handgun if necessary.

The Belly Carry is very popular but not as concealable a position. With this carry, the gun is carried inside the waistband in front of your stomach on one side or the other, usually in the cross-draw position. For some people, it is not as comfortable but access can be as quick as with the Kidney Carry and shorter guns are best suited for this carrying method.

We don't recommend the Shoulder Carry position. It is not as fast as the other carries and can be quite uncomfortable and your draw can be too easily blocked by the arm of an attacker. All the strapping and webbing you have to wear has a tendency to flop around and may cut off circulation and can be very hot in summer months. It has only one advantage over the Kidney or Belly Carry, when drawing from a sitting position it is somewhat easier and faster.

Another carry position is known as the Boot Carry. If you were wearing boots you could use a boot holster which would keep the handgun hidden inside the boot. There are some custom made boots available that have a pouch designed for this type of carry. If you are a right handed shooter the handgun would be kept inside the left boot and vice-versa. As a general rule, this carry is used when carrying more than one handgun. It obviously takes much longer to draw from this position and when faced with a sudden, unexpected attack you would be at a serious disadvantage compared to the other carry positions. You are also limited as far as the type of gun you can carry this way. A small, light frame revolver or a very small compact semi-automatic, such as the Detonic's, would be the only guns powerful enough to carry comfortably and undetected.

When the temperatures allow, a good way to carry is in a jacket or a winter vest pocket. The handgun would have to be lighter than twenty ounces due to the fact that most materials will sag beyond that weight making the gun noticeable. The best handgun for this type of carry would be a five shot alloy frame two inch revolver. The cylinder is smaller making it easier to conceal and the frame is light. The advantage of the pocket carry is that you could have your hand on the weapon and shoot through the pocket if there were no time to draw. You would be limited to using a double action because the safety on a semi-automatic could be jarred to the "off" position creating a hazard. Also, you can't reliably fire a semi-automatic from within a pocket due to jamming and interference from the pocket material when the slide moves. The double action semi-automatic, which we do not prefer for self defense, has the same problem. The revolver you choose, in addition to light weight, should have a shrouded hammer or be modified by de-horning the hammer. When you place the revolver in your pocket, it is important that the barrel be pointed down and slightly forward with the grip at the top of the pocket and slightly to the rear. If you just drop the gun into your pocket, you might find yourself fumbling around for it or get it caught in the lining of the pocket. The biggest advantage of this type of carry is that you can cover someone without their knowledge. If, given a choice and the temperature permits, knowing you would be going into some type of situation which was potentially dangerous, such as a high crime area late at night, we recommend the pocket carry over all others. There is no better way to be ready when undesirable action starts than to have your weapon already in your hand.

Women have an option which most men do not and this is the purse carry. There are purses available from gun equipment manufacturers designed for this purpose. You can, of course, use any purse which can adequately conceal the revolver. We say revolver because, like the pocket carry, a semi-automatic is not advisable in this position. The purse you choose should definitely have a shoulder strap. This is much more secure and harder to snatch. You also don't want to have to hold the purse while reaching for your gun as you would with a clutch type purse. The revolver should be placed in such a position within the purse as to allow for quick, easy access. Preferably you would want the barrel pointing down and slightly forward with the grip pointing up and towards the rear. This will depend on the purse but at the very least the handgun should be horizontal with the sights facing up. You don't want the gun in your purse upside down or unsecured where it can jiggle around so that you don't know which end is up when you reach for it. The advantages of a purse carry are similar to the pocket carry. When going through a dangerous area you can have your hand on the gun and even shoot through the purse if necessary. Also, if you have your hand on the weapon and someone tries to steal your purse he will have drawn your weapon for you. That way a thief may only have your purse and not your gun. Your purse, of course, should be kept on your strong hand side.

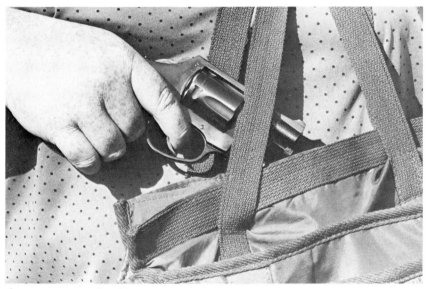

A woman can walk with her hand on the gun while it is still in the purse. She, of course, is ready for instant action.

Drawing

When using the kidney carry and you get the feeling that you might need quick access to your gun, get your strong hand in position for a rapid draw. The best way to place your hand would be on your belt as close as possible to your gun without revealing the gun or your intent. The weak hand should be kept in a ready position to fend off a possible assailant. Make sure that your jacket or other clothing are out of the way so you can freely and clearly draw your weapon if needed. When you draw the gun from the holster with your strong hand, your palm should be facing up so you can correctly grasp the weapon and at the same time use your little finger to keep your clothing out of the way. As you draw the weapon, if the weak hand isn't fending off an assailant, you will be getting into the Weaver stance. Your weak hand should fall into place on the weapon just about waist level. Then, with a thrusting forward motion, if there is time, aim fire or point fire using the top of the barrel. If you are using a semi-automatic, you will have to take off the safety. This should be done after the gun is clear of your body and both hands are positioned on the weapon, out in front of you at about a forty-five degree angle. Your index finger should go into the trigger guard simulteneously or slightly after you remove the safety.

Looking at the intended target, ready to draw.

Little finger of right hand moves inside open vest and starts to sweep vest clear. This move must be smooth and positive. Note that left hand is brought up in position to catch pistol on its way to target.

Right hand has firmly gripped pistol. Note how coat was swept back far enough not to interfere with gripping the pistol.

Pistol is out of holster and on its way to eye level. Left hand is about to catch pistol and assume two hand hold. Note: Do not sweep your left hand with the muzzle.

Pistol is up at eye level and two shots have been fired. Smooth movements and economy of motion bring speed and consistency.

Another way of clearing the outer garment is to use the strong hand thumb and palm.

The palm keeps the vest out of the way while drawing.

The instant the weapon is clear, the weak hand is positioned.

Shooter has now fully gripped the weapon and is ready to fire.

When using the belly carry, your weak hand will be used to get your jacket or other clothing out of the way. You should keep your weak hand elbow against your side and use your weak hand to clear your outer garments. As you draw the gun, your weak hand should be in a position to immediately grasp the weapon. This is the case for both the strong hand draw and the cross draw. If you suspect trouble your hands should be in a ready position, as close to the gun as possible, without exposing the weapon or your intentions.

The shoulder carry, as we have stated, is not recommended. It takes much longer to draw your handgun than the other methods we have described, and it is difficult to be in a good ready position. The shoulder carry will hold the gun too high up on your body for you to inconspicuously lift your outer garments out of the way. If you do use it, you will have to reach in with your strong hand and grasp the gun and use your weak hand, as much as possible, to clear your clothing out of the way. Once you have drawn the gun, your arms will be in a much higher position than with the other carries, so take advantage of this and immediately thrust your weapon forward to fire.

The most critical factor in the pocket carry is having the weapon secured so that it will stay in one position in the pocket. The draw can be very quick and if you are aware of possible danger you can easily have your hand in place already. If the pocket allows you can draw the gun straight out, if not, pull it slightly to the rear and then move the weapon forward. Hold on to the edge of the jacket with your weak hand or the jacket will pull up with the draw. One mistake is trying to thrust towards the target before the gun has fully cleared the pocket and ending up catching it on the garment. Make sure you have a firm grip on the weapon before you draw. If you don't have a firm grip and you catch the barrel on your clothes, you could drop the gun. Once the gun is clear of the pocket thrust forward with a punching motion and fire. If you have to shoot through your pocket, the guidelines of instinct shooting prevail with your strong hand elbow tucked against your side, your forearm parallel to the ground, the barrel pointed at the target and fire. Keep in mind that instinct shooting isn't nearly as accurate as aim or point shooting and is just about useless farther than three to five feet away. If you have enough time it is far better to fully draw your weapon.

As with the pocket carry, maintain consistency in the way you carry and position the handgun in a purse. Every time you reach in the purse you should know exactly where the gun is and shouldn't have to search for it. If the purse has a shoulder strap, which we strongly recommend, when you draw make sure the barrel has cleared it before thrusting forward towards your target. Get a firm grasp on your gun, draw the weapon and drop the purse. Don't worry about the contents of your purse. In such a dangerous situation you don't want to waste motion and time trying to hang onto your purse. The gun should always be

Ready to start the draw.

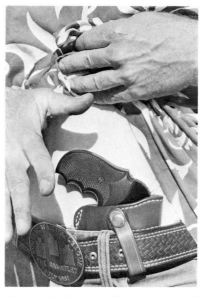

Fingers of left hand lift up shirt while right hand makes a quick but smooth reach for the revolver.

With shirt pulled up, right hand has gripped the revolver. Shirt is held up by left hand till revolver is out of holster and started toward the intended target.

Revolver is on target, ready to fire.

The vest pocket carry.

The hand is in place ready for action.

If time doesn't allow, you can fire through the vest using instinct method.

positioned so that you don't have to use your weak hand to hold onto the purse while drawing your gun. If you have to shoot through the purse the same principles hold true here as when shooting through a pocket.

The Ankle or Boot Carry isn't recommended except in extreme circumstances because you can not draw from this position or even be in a ready position without giving your intentions away. Also, the worst thing you can do is take your eyes off your assailant, and it is very difficult to bend down to draw your weapon without taking your eyes off your target. This type of carry also takes considerably more time to not only draw your weapon but to get into any type of firing stance. With either the Boot or Ankle Carry be sure to wear pants that have a bell or boot flared leg. There are two important reasons for this loose fit; it will help keep the weapon from being detected and will make it considerably easier to clear the pant leg when drawing the weapon.

There are three methods for drawing with the Boot or Ankle Carry. The best overall method is the one foot draw. When facing your target, lift your leg straight up, pull up the pant leg with your weak hand, and draw the weapon. This is the quickest method and allows you to keep your eyes on the target. The disadvantage of this method is that it requires agility on your part.

The bend and draw method doesn't require as much agility. You will bend down, pull up the pant leg with your weak hand, draw the weapon with your strong hand, and bring the gun into firing position. The two disadvantages of this method are; it limits your mobility and can possibly cause you to take your eyes off your assailant. You will remain somewhat mobile, which is not the case with the third method, the squat and roll. This is the poorest method without question. You will squat, grasp the weapon and roll onto your back. As you roll you will bring your weak hand into place on the gun and fire. Your field of vision will be severely diminished and throwing yourself on your back could hurt and disorientate you.

In general, the Ankle or Boot Carry should be used only as a backup or when clothing does not permit another carry. Even as a backup, if your primary weapon has failed, you will have to distract your assailant enough to draw your gun in any way or method that common sense tells you is best for the situation.

Smoothness and economy of motion are critical factors in any type of drawing procedure. It is very important that you have speed and consistency when your life is on the line. The consequences of fumbling or dropping the handgun are very serious. You've got to practice drawing your weapon if you plan to carry it on your person. You never want to take your eyes off the source of trouble and therefore you have to be able to draw without looking at what you're doing. You must practice drawing from the carry position you plan on using. You can practice

When beginning the "one foot draw," shift your weight to your strong leg.

While keeping your eyes on target, the weak hand lifts the pant leg and the strong hand grasps weapon.

In a very short period of time, you are ready to fire and are in perfect position to stand your ground or move.

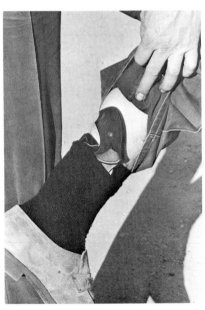

A good ankle holster will be undetectable while standing or moving and must hold the gun securely.

this at home and should also practice live firing after drawing from a concealed carry position at a range. Remember that instinct shooting has an accurate range of only three to five feet and possibly less when firing from inside a pocket or purse and is to be used only when time won't permit aim or point shooting.

You should also practice drawing from an unconcealed position as part of your regular range work. It will help greatly in developing your overall familiarity with your gun.

SPEED RE-LOADING THE D.A. REVOLVER

Push cylinder release and position fingers in preparation for opening.

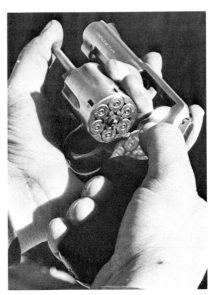

Push open cylinder, hold it firmly and place thumb on ejector rod.

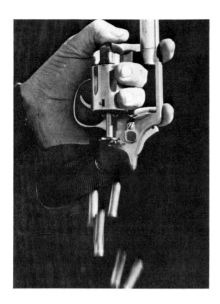

Turn the muzzle "straight up" and then the thumb briskly pushes ejector rod to its bottom position and all spent cases are "ejected." Be sure not to move your arm in a throwing motion. This will impede the ejection process. Also, be certain to check each chamber to be sure none of the cases have somehow stayed in place.

Position your forearm against your side for steadiness and with muzzle pointed downward, guide the cartridges into the chamber. Be sure to hold the cylinder firmly so it doesn't move around.

117

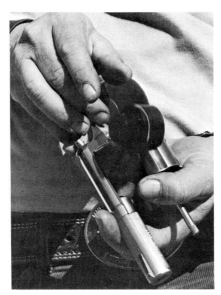

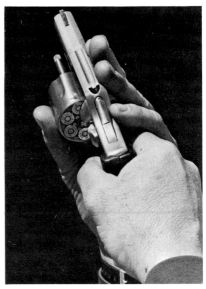

Once you have released the cartridges from the "speed loader," allow it to drop. Note! Don't waste time by throwing it aside; gravity will do the job.

Re-grip and smoothly close cylinder and rotate it until it clicks into place. During this process, you should be beginning to bring the gun back to shooting position.

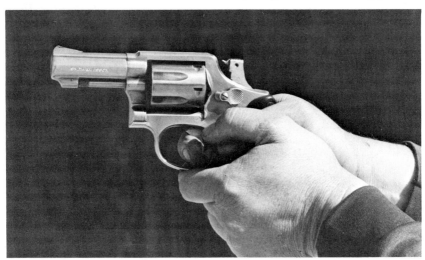

The weapon is now fully loaded. The hands are repositioned and another round is about to be fired. Your goal should be to bring the weapon back into action as fast as possible. Your "out of action" time is from when you decide to reload until you are fully ready to fire after reloading.

SPEED RE-LOADING THE AUTO PISTOL

A quick, smooth reload reduces out of action time. Note: To better illustrate the technique, no coat was worn. Magazine carrier is worn just behind point of left hip with magazine pointing forward. All reload magazines should have base pads.

When beginning reload, safety is left "off" and pistol is twisted slightly in hand allowing thumb to depress magazine release button. Weak hand simultaneously sweeps coat away and grasps fresh magazine.

Spent magazine is falling to ground while fresh magazine is on its way to magazine well.

Pistol is held at eye level while fully loaded magazine is placed heel first into magazine well.

119

Fresh magazine is thrust home in one solid smooth motion with palm and heel of weak hand. Pistol is held high to allow magazine to be "looked" into magazine well. Once this technique is mastered, you can reload without taking your eyes off target.

Once the magazine has been seated into place, the proper grip is re-established and you are ready to fire. Becoming proficient with this skill could save your life.

Index finger of weak hand is positioned along forward edge of magazine just below tip of bullet. Heel of magazine indexes on rear portion of magazine well.

Closeup of weak hand thrusting magazine in magazine well. Notice how strong hand was returned to normal position. The base pad on magazine prevents hand from being pinched and insures proper seating.

An excellent 2″ revolver choice is the Colt Detective Special. High quality has always been a Colt trademark.

CHAPTER 6

LAW AND SELF DEFENSE

By this time, we have to assume you have made the moral choice that you have the right to survive an attack even if it means you may have to kill another human being to do so. Laws concerning self defense vary from state to state. Legislators disagree not only on the value of a human life but also on the topic of victim's rights. We are going to cover only the criminal law aspects, because you should never make a decision to take, or to refrain from taking, another's life based upon mere civil (monetary) liability. We are going to make generalizations which will encompass what most State laws define as a shooting in self defense and also a restatement of general guidelines of when, and when not, to shoot. **We must emphatically state it is your responsibility to educate yourself concerning the particular laws in your state. Do not take it for granted that our generalizations are probably the same as your state's laws merely because they sound logical and reasonable.** The law doesn't always work that way. Most of the specific rules we express are those of the California courts as they are considered a leader in establishing such legal principles.

The threshold question is: What is self defense? A California judge once stated: "When anyone who is not at fault themselves is attacked by another in such a manner or under such circumstances as to furnish reasonable grounds for apprehending a design to take away his life or do him some great bodily harm, and there are reasonable grounds for believing the danger imminent that such a design will be accomplished, then I believe you may act upon appearance and kill the assailant if that be necessary to avoid the apprehended danger."

The killing will be justifiable, although afterwards it may turn out that the appearances were false and there were, in fact, neither design to do one serious injury nor danger that it would be done. A person must

Should she shoot? In this scene, the attacker will decide his own fate. If he continues to move toward her in a life threatening manner or begins to throw the knife at her, she will have to shoot because he is a lethal threat. If he suddenly turns to run or drops his weapon and freezes, she would not shoot. At this point, he would no longer be a lethal threat; there would be no justification to fire in self defense.

decide at his peril upon the course of the circumstances in which he is placed.

You don't need proof positive that someone intended to kill you; you don't have to sustain a wound before you can act. You are justified in **acting upon appearances** where you exercise your common sense. If someone walks toward you, points a gun in your direction and threatens you with death, you don't have to let him get off the first shot before you can defend yourself. You can act upon appearances and believe the gun is indeed loaded, and you can fire first. It may later turn out the gun was unloaded or the person was playing a morbid joke, but you were justified in firing to protect yourself against imminent danger. You must also be aware of the possibility that a jury may decide whether or not you had reasonable grounds for your actions so, again, use your common sense. We would rather face a jury of twelve peers than six feet of dirt.

A child with a water pistol, on the other hand, is most likely **not** a danger to your life. Obviously, as the following actual case history will show, you have to take that split second to make sure you are indeed in imminent danger and justified in acting upon appearances. You can not blindly rush in and shoot at anything that moves or seems out of place.

Steven Hiatt, a twenty-seven year old man from Colorado, shot and killed a nine year old girl who ran into his apartment. She was playing with friends and was not accustomed to knocking before entering a room, because her parents were deaf. When she ran into the man's apartment, he was in his bedroom and thought he heard an intruder. He then grabbed his gun and shot the girl in the head.

He did not take that split second to make sure he was in imminent danger and to identify his target. He panicked and recklessly shot at the first thing he saw when he entered his living room. He was **not** acting upon appearances.

Lethal force is a key phrase in a **justifiable** self defense shooting. Lethal will be defined as that which is fatal or pertains to death. Force, obviously, is that which provides the catalyst. There are very few inanimate objects which would not, under any circumstances, be considered incapable of providing lethal force. Even a pillow can be used to suffocate someone. The human body has many vulnerable areas, and certainly a punch to a vital part from a powerful person can cause instant death. As a result, there are a great many variables which constitute lethal force in a self defense situation.

A great difference in size and learned or physical capabilities are factors to consider if you are attacked by an unarmed person. A one hundred and twenty pound woman could be killed with the bare fists of a two hundred pound man. She may be justified in defending herself with a weapon based upon his obvious physical advantage over her. On the other hand, if the positions were reversed, and she threatened to smother him with a pillow, he wouldn't have much of a defense if he shot and killed her claiming the pillow in her hands was a lethal weapon.

If an attacker has a black belt in karate or is a boxer, you are not automatically entitled to use lethal force against him unless the person has a history of using his skills with intent to injure people. Lethal is therefore, a combination of capability and intent.

When we teach our self defense courses, many students ask the question: "How close do I have to let an attacker get before I can shoot?" By reading between the lines it is apparent they aren't asking so much about when they should shoot; but are instead admitting that fear would dictate their response to a threat rather than confidence in their abilities. Fear is panic, and panic can result in reckless reactions. It can be overcome through the confidence that comes from pre-planning and diligent practice. By learning how to use your weapon effectively, and the variety of weapons and types of attacks that can be used against you, you will be better prepared to know at what moment to "drop the hammer." This knowledge will tell you that a man more than twenty yards away from you, armed with a knife, is not capable of harming you, even though he may seem intent on throwing the knife at that distance. It will tell you that the same man at the same distance armed with a

125

small derringer would need tremendous luck to even wound you, much less kill you.

Those may seem like clear cut examples. Let's say you are a one hundred pound woman and a two hundred pound man approaches you on the street and begins to threaten you from a distance of twenty feet. He is only seconds away from being on top of you. He appears to possess the capability of lethal force by his size alone, and he seems intent on using it against you. But, until he gets closer or displays a weapon he can not, at that distance, use that lethal force. The problem is if you shot him at a distance of twenty feet you could only prove he threatened you verbally and that isn't enough. Paranoid fear is not a good enough reason to justify lethal force. **Reasonable fear is!** He must instill you with a reasonable fear, through his actions, such as displaying a weapon or advancing on you in an aggressive manner. We are not saying you can not stand ready, or you have to allow him to actually grab you; but you must have a reasonable fear a deadly attack is imminent before you fire.

You have to use your common sense and not over-react. The danger to you must be imminent. You can't use lethal force against someone who has merely threatened you in the past, or made a future or conditional threat. Imminent danger is something which is immediately threatening; danger which is about to befall. Your life must be in danger at that very moment before you can use lethal force.

If you are still wondering how to decide who is a threat and who isn't, here are a couple of examples. If someone is more than twenty yards away with a handgun, you'd be better off, from a legal standpoint, to give him the opportunity to give up or run than to shoot him. Anyone within a few steps of you is a potential lethal threat. Anyone with a long gun (shotgun or rifle) is the most dangerous threat. If you honestly feel your life is in danger from anyone, save your life first. No citizen can or should be expected to forfeit his own life in favor of the life of his assailant.

HOW SHOULD YOU REACT TO A NON-LETHAL ATTACK?

None of us likes to be harrassed by a group of punks or some unfortunate individual who acts in a deranged and insulting manner. None of us wants our spouse flirted with especially in our presence. But, these situations are never a reason for you to threaten to use or to actually use lethal force. You are expected as a gun owner to use more than normal restraint at times. It may be ego deflating, but it does not give you the right to escalate the situation. **Remember non-lethal force against a non-lethal threat and lethal force against a lethal threat.** Even if your life is verbally threatened, you can not use a weapon unless you reasonably believe your life is in danger at that very moment. We all know our limits emotionally and, for most of us, it is far better to swallow our pride than to allow a situation to escalate from a minor incident to a major one. Should the situation escalate and you draw your weapon against someone who is not armed, you now possess the far greater force, and should there be a shooting, your claim of self defense would be weak or even non-existent.

If you are punched, most of the time, you can punch back. If someone appears to go for a weapon, or has produced one, you can draw yours. If someone attempts to use a weapon against you, you can use yours. If it appears you escalated the situation which resulted in a shooting, you are in for serious legal problems.

As an adult, you are legally expected to exercise reasonable restraint. If you have, on your person, a handgun you are really expected to exercise, what most of us would feel is, more than reasonable restraint. Our pride and egos are not important enough, either morally or legally, to be considered a part of our vital life support system. They mend very easily.

We have mentioned that even a pillow or the human hand can be considered lethal force. There is no way of knowing if someone is a professional boxer or a martial arts expert, and you certainly can't wait to find out the hard way by allowing an unarmed person to get close enough to do you serious damage. You have no way of knowing whether or not your attacker will draw a weapon. In this type of situation, there are two considerations, the legal aspects and your right to survive. Legally you can't wave your weapon in a threatening manner at an unarmed person. Basically you don't want to put yourself in the position of having to explain your actions to the police should this person go to them and complain that you threatened him with a gun. Chances are this wouldn't happen, because he would also have to explain what action on his part caused you to do this. But, in general it's not a good idea to display your weapon in a threatening manner unless someone is honestly threatening your life. You may have honestly felt you were being threatened and displayed your weapon as a deterrent, but things have a way of "snow-balling" and your local District Attorney may be pro-gun control and decide to make an example of you.

If you have legally registered your gun and, with witnesses, your testimony and your attacker's background verify you were in real danger, then you have a chance. But, if for some reason your gun wasn't registered or you have no witnesses, you could have a real legal nightmare on your hands. It is a rare situation, as we stated before, where someone with a criminal background who threatened you initially would then lodge a complaint against you. But, very possibly you could find yourself in this situation because a witness to the incident telephoned the police. So, we urge you to exercise restraint before drawing your weapon because your assailant isn't going to tell the police, "Yes, officer, I just attempted to commit a crime. Charge me. The person with the gun is innocent."

This probably sounds like you're damned if you do and possibly dead if you don't. There are many different types of people in this world. Some may only intend to threaten you and others may intend to do more. If someone threatens you, you can't play the odds and there isn't time to get an opinion from your local District Attorney's office. You have to make a decision that your life is threatened based on your attacker's actions, physical capabilities, and whether he poses a lethal threat at that very moment. You must be ready, from a tactical standpoint, to use your weapon either as a deterrent or for self defense. If he continues to threaten you, you have no other choice but to defend yourself. If he backs down and/or leaves, you are in the clear. If the police miraculously show up when you have drawn a weapon, expect a problem. It will probably be your word against your attacker's, but at least you're still around to give your version.

A threat is not lethal force! If we were to shoot someone everytime we were threatened, most of us would have probably killed at least one person by the time we reached our twenties. Telling a judge, "but he threatened me and had a knife!" might not stand up in court if you had a gun, knew how to use it, and did use it, without giving your assailant an opportunity to put down his weapon or escape, or at least back down from his threat. You are probably saying, "Why should I let this person escape? He may cause harm to someone else and doesn't belong on the street." Your response may be an accurate appraisal of the situation, but the law doesn't usually allow you to detain someone with the use of lethal force. If your assailant gives up and you turn him over to the police, that is fine. But, in most states, if you were to shoot him to prevent him from escaping you would be charged criminally, and possibly sued civilly, for wrongful death. This could hold true even if the assailant is leaving with some of your personal possessions. In any case, your right to self defense ends when the attacker attempts to escape, even if the attacker is still armed. If you were to decide to exact vengeance on this person by tracking him down, cornering and forcing him into a fight, you would then be the aggressor and the initial attacker would have the right to self defense. As a general principle, you can rely upon the rule that deadly force can be used against a deadly attack and non-deadly force against a non-deadly attack. If you are the original aggressor, or escalate a non-lethal confrontation into a lethal stage, then you do not have the right to self defense unless you communicate at some point an absolute desire to abandon the attack. The following case will illustrate the concepts of retreat, escape, escalating an attack, and communicating the desire to abandon the attack.

Two men, Mr. Smith and Mr. Jones, had the same girlfriend. Mr. Smith went to Mr. Jones' house and broke in armed with a knife. He then attacked Mr. Jones, who was on his couch. They fought and since Mr. Jones was bigger, he disarmed Mr. Smith. Jones then proceeded to beat Smith. Smith regained the knife and started to run through the house looking for another way out. He was finally cornered by Jones in a hallway. Jones then proceeded to beat Smith again. Mr. Smith defended himself with the knife and justifiably killed Jones.

If Mr. Smith, the original aggressor, had run through the house only to find a better position in which to launch a second attack, he would have had no right to self defense. However, he had entirely abandoned the original attack and sought only to escape, so he acquired the right to self defense. Mr. Jones had given up his original right to the same by pursuing a fleeing Smith with the intention of exacting vengeance on him.

Assuming the worst, for whatever reason you could not escape, you now have to decide if the attacker has both the capability and intention of causing you deadly harm. This is a vital judgement that must often be made in a matter of split seconds. If you know the attacker doesn't have the capability, or you aren't sure and are not in immediate danger, then you have to wait until you are sure before you can take action. Acting when you aren't sure could result in manslaughter charges being brought against you.

Manslaughter is defined as an unlawful killing, with intent to kill but without malice aforethought. Essentially, it is an intentional killing with an unjustifiable, unreasonable response to the victim's provocation. This is a situation where someone over-reacted. A "victim" started a fist fight and, while punching the defendant, the defendant over-reacted to the provocation and shot him. If you shot someone who was pointing a stick at you, that would be manslaughter due to extreme paranoia and over-reaction on your part. You intended to kill and did so unreasonably, but there were mitigating factors such as provocation. Being aware of your surroundings, pre-planning and practice will give you sufficient confidence in your ability to instantly defend yourself so as to prevent over-reaction. This should keep you from facing manslaughter charges. Knowing you have practiced enough with your weapon to fire instantly and hit, will allow you enough time to take in information before you "drop the hammer."

Up to this point, we have been mostly talking in terms of a one-on-one attack. If there are more than one assailant, other factors come into play. Unless you are a tremendously strong person, two male assailants or even one male and one female assailant can constitute deadly force whether or not they are armed. You still have to be sure in your mind that they are capable, and intend to use deadly force, and you should generally try to escape or allow them the opportunity to escape and abandon the attack. If no escape is possible and the danger appears to be imminent, you have the right to defend yourself against any member of the group who, by their actions, appear to be a lethal threat. Obviously, from a tactical standpoint, you should decide who poses the most danger and take care of that individual first. Any remaining member of the group of assailants who continues to be a lethal threat should also be stopped.

The situation could arise in which a survivor (or survivors) of the group is so stunned at the sight of his or her accomplice's death he abandons his own attack. As long as he or she poses no threat and does not continue to act in a life threatening manner, you can not shoot and you can not detain them with lethal force. Even though they initially acted as a group, you can not hold them all liable for each other's actions. You could shoot and kill the first assailant in self defense legally, and end up being charged with the shooting of a second member of the group who was turning to flee or posed no threat after his accomplice's downfall.

You may be wondering how you will be able to ascertain whether or not the other members of the group are a lethal threat. Your practice and pre-planning will help you immensely to be observant and to react in a calm calculating manner.

An often discussed issue is **whether you can stand your ground in a confrontation or must turn and run.** If you can safely avoid a confrontation by all means, do it. California law says you can stand your ground wherever you are. However, a number of states say you can **never** stand your ground. You must always try to escape and secondly allow the attacker to escape. This will be critical in any self defense hearing in a state with this law. You must prove there was no alternative to the confrontation. Then there are other states where you are allowed to stand your ground if you are on your own property but not allowed to do so if you are on public property. You should check with a local criminal lawyer to ascertain if you have legal right to stand your ground or whether your state believes you owe your attacker a shot at your back while you run. If it is the latter, we would **move to another state.**

Should you ever defend someone else, such as a stranger, who appears to be under attack in the street? The right to act upon appearances comes into play here. You do have the right to stop a felony from being committed and the right to act upon what appears to be a lethal threat. But, what if you were wrong about who was the aggressor? We recommend you don't act upon appearances in this type of situation and instead call the police. You could be seen as a vigilante who goes around looking for a fight. Protect yourself and your loved ones, but unless you are absolutely sure, don't get involved in confrontations between strangers. The following case will demonstrate the fine line you must walk to protect others.

Mrs. Williams had some property at the victim's house she wanted to recover. She and her sister went to the house armed with handguns.

Mrs. Williams went inside and her sister stayed outside. Mrs. Williams pulled her gun on the victim. The victim struggled with her and took the gun from Mrs. Williams. The victim simply wanted to disarm her and stop the threat and had no intention of using the weapon on Mrs. Williams. Mrs. Williams screamed to her sister, who was outside and hadn't seen what had happened, "Help me! He's got a gun and is going to kill me!" Her sister ran inside and killed the victim.

Her sister had acted upon appearances and was charged with but later found not guilty of murder even though she had fired the gun. Mrs. Williams **was** found guilty of the victim's murder because she had caused the death of the victim by "setting him up" to be shot, and because she was the original aggressor with no right to self defense.

THE NEGLIGENT SHOOTING OF A BYSTANDER

What happens if you shoot at an attacker and miss and hit an innocent bystander? You are generally not **criminally** liable if you acted in a reasonable manner and were not **grossly** negligent. You have the right to defend yourself but not with reckless disregard for the safety of others. Panic can cause you to become reckless. If you hit someone ninety feet to your left when the assailant was right in front of you, or you manage to hit the assailant but kept firing as you waved your gun around, you were both reckless and negligent as well as incompetent. Practicing with your weapon is one way of insuring you do not panic. Learn to hit what you shoot at and learn to stop an attacker with two or three shots. This is not only your best chance for successfully defending yourself but also for safeguarding bystanders.

You do have the right to prevent a felony. When we say felony, please bear in mind that we are talking about a violent crime such as rape, murder, kidnapping and armed robbery. Writing a bad check for over five hundred dollars is a felony but certainly doesn't justify lethal force. When your life is threatened by someone committing a felony, then you can and should defend yourself.

There are several crimes besides attempted murder which justify self defense with lethal force, such as rape and arson. In the case of arson we can only give you a generalization; check the laws which apply in your area. If you saw someone committing arson by attempting to set an apartment house on fire, generally you would be justified in using lethal force should the arsonist refuse to stop what he was doing. Arson involves more than the destruction of property. It can also destroy people. If you caught the arsonist after the fire had been set, you would not be justified in shooting him. This would be an after the fact shooting, and you could be criminally liable.

In the case of rape this would, for the most part, involve a man against a woman. We have discussed disparity of force due to a difference in size and in most cases the woman would be at a severe dis-

A lethal threat is clearly present and imminent danger is facing the armed citizen. The intruder has been ordered to "freeze" but has responded by trying to move his weapon at the defender. The justification to shoot in self defense is very clear, but you must be prepared to prove your actions were correct.

advantage. A woman would be justified in using lethal force if necessary to prevent a rape. She would not be justified in shooting her attacker after the attack unless her attacker continued to lethally threaten her. But, before and during, the woman has every right to use lethal force to stop the attack.

The law, in most states, allows you to defend your property but common sense tells us to only defend your life. Belongings can be replaced, but a life can't. You can't shoot at a fleeing thief unless he is shooting while fleeing and still presenting a life endangering threat. **When the threat is gone, so is your justification.** As a general rule, never shoot at someone who is leaving the scene. If someone is holding a knife on you while they attempt to steal your television, then you have the right to defend yourself and incidentally, your property. The only time you can defend property is when your life is also in danger.

You can't set a trap gun. Some people have gone so far as to wire a gun to go off in the event of a burglary. This is not only foolish but dangerous and illegal. How would you feel if you caused a fireman or a police officer to sustain a gunshot wound because they attempted to enter your home or business?

If you are in your home or place of business and you own a properly registered gun, you generally have the right to carry it on your person. If

132

someone takes it upon himself to break into your home, by that act alone, you can assume the confrontation will involve lethal force. You can not afford to assume that the intruder is unarmed. Some states, however, won't allow you to step outside your front door with your weapon.

Most of us hope never to have to face an intruder who breaks in while we are at home but many of us will find ourselves a victim of burglary while we were away. There is always the possibility when you arrive home an intruder may still be there and become aware of your presence. Your first action would be to leave and call the police from someplace else rather than to enter your home to investigate. What happens if you have to face this intruder in your yard? First, you should try to leave or allow him to leave. A shoot out in your yard isn't a very good idea and should be avoided if possible. Don't shoot in anger or try to provoke the intruder. If you can, place yourself behind cover and, order the individual to halt. If he doesn't appear to be leaving and starts firing at you, then you would be justified in returning fire. Self defense means exactly what it says. It does not mean you can escalate the confrontation or take an **offensive** position. You can not become the aggressor unless you are forced into a position where you must defend yourself.

Carrying a concealed weapon is allowed, in many states, in your place of business and at your residence. Generally, if you want to carry a gun with you on the street, you must have a permit. Most states require this. The specific requirements and the number of permits issued vary greatly from state to state and even from county to county. We can make a few generalizations here which would be helpful, but we advise you to find out what laws and requirements apply where you live. Permits to carry a weapon are generally not honored outside of your own state. If you travel, most likely, you won't be able to carry your weapon into another state on your person.

Most states allow you to carry an unloaded weapon in your car trunk but check with your local Police Department. If you don't have a trunk and you decide to transport your weapon anyway, then it would be a good idea to make sure it is not visible to anyone looking in your car windows. We think it is a bad idea to ever leave your gun in a visible place in your car and this includes having it in a gun bag which is visible. Almost everyone, especially the police, knows what a gun bag looks like and what is usually carried in one. If you get stopped for a ticket, you will definitely be delayed and have to do some explaining. Many people carry their weapon in the glove compartment or a center console. They keep their car registration clipped to the visor so they won't have to search through these compartments looking for it and accidently expose the weapon.

If you are carrying a weapon which is not visible and you get stopped, you do not have to tell the officer you have a gun or let him search your car. A police officer must have probable cause to search your car. **Without a search warrant, you don't have to allow him to search.** By 'allow' we mean giving him your permission. As a practical matter, you can't literally prevent a law officer from searching; but you don't have to give your permission by saying it's alright with you if he searches. Anything an officer may find as a result of an illegal search cannot be used as evidence against you. An illegal search is one made without your permission and without cause to believe you have committed a crime.

What if you actually have to shoot someone? First of all, you should have practiced enough to have attained a degree of efficiency which will allow you to stop an assailant with two or three shots. You don't want to empty your gun into an assailant unless it's absolutely necessary. Tactically, you could be faced with more than one assailant and reloading takes up valuable time. Legally it doesn't look good if you have emptied your gun because it could appear that you panicked, were overly zealous, or even murderous in the way you reacted. You can only fire to **stop** the attack. Conceptually, if you fired six rounds, reloaded and shot six more, somewhere along the line, before you fired that last shot, you stopped the attack. You can not shoot a man on the ground who is unable to return fire, even if he deserves it. Self defense is not killing an attacker, it is stopping an attack. The attacker may die, but that is not the reason why you shoot in self defense. **You shoot to stop!**

Surviving the battle is only the first step; now you must survive the aftermath. The first thing you should do after the crisis has subsided is call the police and an ambulance. Tell the police you are armed and what you look like. Always protect and preserve any evidence. If one of the gang members removes the weapon an assailant tried to use against you, you have lost valuable evidence needed to justify your shooting in self defense. There is a case where this happened. Five members of a gang tried to assault a man who defended himself and killed one of the gang members. Somehow, in the confusion, one of the remaining gang members took the gun and it vanished. They denied there ever was any weapon. The man who shot in self defense was convicted but, fortunately, his sentence was overturned when one of the gang members later confessed.

Also, try to get all witnesses names and the license plate numbers of their cars before they leave the scene. Most people are willing to talk and help you immediately after witnessing a crime. Later they might change their minds and decide not to come forward out of fear. If you know who they are and get them to give a statement right away, you won't have the problem of tracking down reluctant witnesses later.

If you have to pick up the weapon to guard it, remember not to get your fingerprints all over it. Pick it up by the slide or the barrel, not the grip. This will not only preserve the evidence but also, while waiting for the police to arrive, will make sure that another member of the gang can't use it against you. When the police arrive, don't make the mistake of still standing there with your weapon drawn; holster it. If you are in possession of an evidence weapon have it laying at your feet, not in your hand. Identify yourself and let the police disarm you. Never attempt to hand your weapon to a police officer, because you just may panic him into shooting you. You don't want to be the victim of mistaken identity.

This is not the time to strike up a conversation or try to make friends with the police. Any statement given to the police can be used against you. You may have been obviously justified, but their job is not always in your best interest. They are there to gather and preserve evidence and you are now part of that evidence. You have just undergone severe stress and may not be thinking as clearly as you normally would. You don't want to risk saying the wrong thing. You must also realize you will not be able to talk your way out of being taken to the police station. At the very least, you will be held for questioning. Many people make the mistake of thinking they can convey to the police they have done nothing wrong and are a law abiding citizen and avoid further interrogation. This can only make matters worse. The police will undoubtably ask you, at the scene, about what happened. Don't try to explain anything until you have talked to your attorney. Simply inform the police you will answer any questions **after** you have talked to your attorney. It is advisable to have an attorney you can call or have a friend find one for you. If you can't do either of these, then you may have to wait in jail for a court appointed attorney. If the press are present, please **don't** say anything to them as well. They are known to sensationalize and get something blown all out of proportion, and you certainly don't need this on top of everything else.

After a shooting, if it is safe, you have made sure the area is clear and the assailant is no longer a threat, call an ambulance. From a humane standpoint you should call one and from a legal standpoint it looks better. Once you have saved your life, you should be concerned enough to call an ambulance for the individual who attacked you.

Handguns, as we have stated, are probably used most often in self defense situations as a deterrent. We must make it absolutely clear that a handgun is always considered lethal force. You can not wave your gun at someone to make him stop what they are doing unless their actions are threatening your life. We hope it is also obvious you should never shoot to disarm or wound, you must realize any shot can kill. If it isn't a situation in which you would be justified in killing, then you have no business using your weapon. However, when justified, you are shooting to stop the attack, not to kill. A death is often an unavoidable result.

We do not recommend you try to make a citizen's arrest or try to prevent someone from leaving the scene of an accident or crime. If you want to play policeman, join the police force. Never put yourself in jeopardy and always exercise your common sense. Don't try to be a hero.

Self defense means in defense of your self not your property or your pride. We strongly urge you to accept the responsibility and take the time to learn how to use your weapon, and when to use it, in accordance with the local laws in your area.

The California Supreme Court once stated, "Men would not quit the freedom of a state of nature and tie themselves up under a government, were it not to preserve their lives, liberty, and fortunes. It cannot be supposed that they should intend to give anyone an absolute power over their persons and estates. For this were to put them in a worse condition than a state of nature, wherein they had the liberty to defend their rights against the injuries of others."

While it is impossible for us to advocate you disregard the law in the name of self defense, we must acknowledge the interpretations of these laws aren't always sensible. It is easier to survive a court battle than wounds from a gunshot or an edged weapon. **As a responsible adult, it is up to you to be fully aware of the laws in your area and the choices you must make.**

WHAT NO ONE WANTS TO HEAR

Self defense manuals, whether they concern martial arts or any number of other techniques, fail to explain what to expect should you injure or kill another person. Most people don't consider this emotional aspect a part of self defense but rather as an insignificant after effect. This attitude is unrealistic. Just as lightning can strike twice, despite popular belief, you could be the victim of an attack more than once. How you handle the after shock of an attack will affect your reactions and ability to defend yourself in the future.

Again, the need for thorough preplanning and practice is absolutely necessary to assure yourself that you took all precautions and acted in a responsible manner when confronted. It is much less traumatic an event to deal with if you don't have to second guess yourself the rest of your life.

There is a psychological reaction to any act of violence. This effect may make itself felt immediately through tears, nausea and trembling. Many times, though, the effect is not so swift and may take days, weeks, even months to be felt. It is common to dwell on unpleasant events long after the actual occurrence, and you may find yourself reviewing the experience and reassessing what you did and what you might have done differently. Unless you are prepared for this reaction and are able to respond appropriately, it could adversely affect your life.

We have discussed the stress of a lethal confrontation but at no time is the strain more evident than afterwards. During a confrontation you may not be consciously aware of many things which are happening around you because you are acting on your instinctive survival drive and are focusing on trying to stay alive. This will block your awareness of the stress you are experiencing at the time. When the crisis subsides, regardless of whether or not you acted correctly in your own self defense, or to save another, you will feel the impact of this stress. Distress may actually be a more definitive term for what you may find yourself feeling.

It is hard to predict exactly how each individual will react after an experience like this, but there are certain common responses such as:

Depersonalization: "I don't believe this happened to me. This can't be real "

Confusion: "What is going on here?"

Time distortion: Time may appear to have slowed down.

Guilt: "I'm so sorry. Forgive me."

Anger: "Why did he make me do this!"

Fear: "The worst thing I ever expected has happened to me, and I don't think I'll ever feel safe again."

If you are forced to kill someone, you are likely to feel that you have done something wrong. It may have been a no choice situation but deep down you may question the morality of your actions. You may experience grief or a feeling of sadness. Many people feel shaky and somehow threatened for a while especially when the police and the press are present, because they feel they may have violated some sort of code. Denying these feelings by detaching yourself from emotional responses may cause you to manifest them physically such as an upset stomach, nervousness, headaches, an unusually quick temper or develop problems with sleeping.

You must, as soon as possible, sit down with the realization that a serious thing has happened in your life and acknowledge how you are feeling about it and how you are going to deal with it. Denying your feelings or delaying the necessity of confronting this reality could develop into a larger problem.

Keeping your perspective realistic is difficult when your life has gone through such a major upheaval. Police officers are more likely to have experienced just such a situation and many of them have reported also having difficulties dealing with this event in their lives. Some have become obsessive about their actions to the extent that they feel "everyone knows what I've done." They report feeling depressed, lousy, and ill though without any real illness. These are, of course, extreme anxiety types of reactions and probably due in large part to pressure from fellow officers to live up to an unrealistic image of themselves.

Other people who may appear to have gone through this experience without any adverse reactions have all of a sudden announced, "I can't face the possibility that this could happen again so I'm getting rid of my gun." They have decided to become a possible dead martyr rather than defend their lives in a similar situation where shooting someone might be the only option.

Stressful situations occur suddenly and the person may view them as somehow his or her fault. The guilt many people feel is expressed very directly such as "I did something wrong or this wouldn't have happened to me." This is a natural response and is a result of the need to regain the feeling you have some control over your life. For most of us talking about it and questioning ourselves is the first step in coping with such an event. You need to understand what happened and why by "getting it out of your system." The easiest way to do this is by talking and reviewing your actions.

Many people seem to have successfully dealt with this experience but find they still think back on the incident unexpectedly. With time this will become less frequent and less vivid. There are numerous ways we might react to a crisis, and we have listed some of the more common reactions.

Anger	Frustration
Anxiety	Guilt
Confusion	Headaches
Crying spells	Laughing/Joking
Denial	Nightmares
Depression	Panic
Disbelief	Calm
Distrust	Shock
Fear	Sympathy for the Attacker

How well we deal with the after effects of a shooting will depend on how well we prepare ourselves for the possibility in the first place. Practicing with your weapon and preplanning for a confrontation to the extent you know that you acted exactly as you should have will help you immensely if you find yourself facing self doubt after an incident. During your preplanning exercises, you might want to seriously evaluate your responses to this type of situation. Try fantasizing an actual incident where you must decide whether or not you are capable of taking a life to save your own or those of your family's. You must be sure you can follow through before you find yourself in an actual situation. If you think that you wouldn't defend yourself, then you most likely are better off without a weapon. You will not only face certain death from a criminal who will turn your own weapon on you, but you will also add to a criminal's arsenal. If you believe you can go through with such an action, then take some time to think about what kind of a reaction you might have afterwards.

Unless you are an extremely unfeeling person, you must realize you will be affected emotionally. You may feel many of the emotions we have described and this is both normal and healthy. Taking another life is traumatic, but you can come out of such an experience a stronger person if you realize beforehand what you may feel and decide how you are going to deal with it. You will realize your life is of more value than someone who is willing to take it from you. You can emerge with a more realistic perspective of how serious life is and with a more mature attitude towards life and your right to it.

The Charter Arms "Bulldog" has effective stopping power in a very compact size. The .44 special cartridge is a real powerhouse. It is best suited for average to larger built individuals.

Shooting skills must be supported by common sense tactical approaches to self defense situations. Careful preparation can enhance your ability to survive.

CHAPTER 7

TACTICS

Tactics for self defense require your full understanding. They are designed for the purpose of survival and in no way are they applicable for arrest or apprehension. On the contrary, we strongly advise against any citizen attempting to capture anyone; this should be left to the police. Putting yourself in unnecessary jeopardy constitutes going against everything this book is about. Taking an offensive position for any purpose other than self defense will put your life in unwarranted jeopardy. It is your responsibility to use the tactics we recommend with common sense. This includes being realistic about the physical or psychological limitations you might possess.

The tactics we will be discussing must be practiced, and they must become an integral part of your preplanning. Don't just read this chapter, **memorize it!** If you should become involved in a deadly confrontation, nine times out of ten, you will not have the time to think, only time to react. Through practice and preplanning you will subconsciously react in the decisive manner that is the key to survival.

Before detailing what to do, we think you should be aware of the many things you shouldn't do. First, you never shoot to wound or disarm; you shoot to stop. Regardless of how good a shooter you might feel you are, or how safe a position you command, there is no sensible reason for shooting to disarm. Although the idea is a humane one, shooting to disarm from a tactical standpoint is very dangerous. More than likely, you will only give the attacker the opportunity to return fire or allow him time and warning to seek cover or concealment. Even the best marksman would have an extremely hard time trying to accomplish this task, because the target is such a small moving one. Don't be fooled by the movies where they show a police officer shooting to disarm. Police are in fact trained to shoot to stop as well. This is another dangerous myth Hollywood has originated.

Never fire a warning shot in a self defense situation. You will waste ammunition, alert the attacker as to your position and the fact you are armed, and send the bullet you just shot who knows where. Never fire your weapon anywhere but at your target. Many police departments throughout the country are now advising against their officers firing warning shots for both tactical reasons, as well as a public safety measure. Concerning the wasting of ammunition, always realize that should a confrontation be extended, you could dearly need that wasted round.

No matter how much control you feel you might have gained in a self defense situation, never relax or take your eyes off the attacker. The advantage you might have can be lost in an instant. Regardless of how disabled the attacker appears, whether he has surrendered or is wounded, never relax to the point where you may give him a second chance to attack you. You may think he's disarmed, but he could be concealing another weapon or faking the extent of his injuries. You can't trust someone who has just tried to violently attack you.

Don't escalate the situation. You can cause an escalation in a couple of ways. The first is to hunt down an intruder. Not only are you increasing your chances of an actual confrontation taking place, but you lose the advantages of surprise and time you could be using to place yourself in a barricaded position. The second way you could escalate a situation is by letting your emotions rule your actions. You might have brought the situation under control and now have a docile attacker, but you "blow it" by allowing your anger to take over. You may very well want to tell this person off, but by doing so you may allow yourself to become distracted, or you could entice the controlled intruder into attacking you by antagonizing him.

Don't ever underestimate the skills of an attacker. The hardened criminal is often an expert in his field. Even disarmed he is capable of causing you great harm if you are not cautious. Don't try to reason with an attacker with the hope you can talk your way out of the situation. This is not the time to practice your diplomacy or try to play the role of a social worker. It is a time to act in a decisive manner to ensure your survival.

We have mentioned some things you should not do because these are the things you need to be aware of first, before you can understand the psychology involved in tactics. Many people, who have no experience with a handgun, have adopted erroneous attitudes which need to be corrected. Many of us have a tendency to relax after a crisis has subsided. **This could be very dangerous!!** Most of us have probably underestimated a social or business situation and a mistake in these situations will probably not cost us our lives, but in a deadly confrontation it could. A self defense situation differs radically from other situations and is one many of you have never experienced. Too many people rely on their image of themselves. They think they will remain cool and calm under this type of pressure. It is imperative to realize that unless you preplan your actions and fully understand all aspects of tactics, you probably won't react in the cool and calm way that you hope you will. This is the most extreme pressure you will ever find yourself under, and you have the opportunity now to think about what you would do and to prepare yourself for this possibility. We would not want to stake our lives on our egos when we have a method available which will help us prepare for our survival. Laziness is a poor excuse for death.

TACTICS IN THE HOME

It is easy to fall victim to a false sense of security once we enter our homes and lock the doors. We tend to act as if once we are in our home nothing can harm us. Quite to the contrary, statistics have shown you are more likely to be the victim of a murderous assault in the home. You can make your home far more secure by utilizing the security measures we will discuss such as alarms, etc. They can give you precious extra time to put your preplanning and tactical approaches into effect.

The first step is to tactically map out your home. Plan it on paper but engrave it in your memory. You want to note all possible entrances, exits, areas which have shadows, and any areas which can be used for cover or concealment. If this is done properly, you will never waste time deciding what to do or where to go. More than likely, you will also have a good idea where an intruder might be headed or hiding. Your main goal would be to avoid a confrontation, but if that isn't possible, to find the best cover or concealment you can use to your advantage. When preplanning take into consideration every room, the best place to be positioned, and the time factor involved in getting into position. We know of many people who have arranged their furniture to be not only fashionable but also tactically favorable.

Ideally in any room you should designate the position which provides the best cover or concealment. This spot will be placed as far away from the entrance as possible. One reason is an assailant entering the room from that entrance would be too far away from you to effectively use instinct firing, five to ten feet. This would also place you far enough away so you wouldn't have to engage in a hand to hand struggle.

In your tactical mapping, you want to preplan for every possible encounter with an intruder from every possible angle. Keep in mind other members of the household and where they sleep, or where they are the most likely to be located. Anyone living in your home, with the exception of infants and very young children, should be aware of the tactical plan and know how to carry out his role in that plan. Whether it's simply a matter of instructing your children about basic security such as keeping certain doors locked and where to assemble if something should occur, it all must be preplanned.

To help you lay out your tactical preplanning map let's use the living room in this diagram as an example.

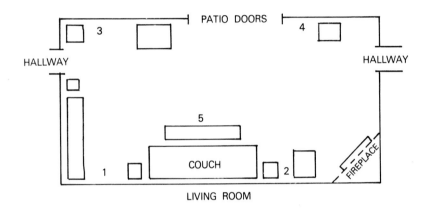

Area number five would be a terrible choice because you have three points of possible entry from which an assailant can launch an attack and you are in the open. Areas three and four would be a slightly better choice but still have drawbacks. Both of these areas place you between two entrances and could put you perilously close to an attacker entering from these areas. You are also at an awkward angle to watch all the entrances. The best choice would be areas one or two. Which one would be best would be determined by the amount of concealment each offered and, if known, the location of the intruder.

A bedroom is another room that requires particularly careful attention. Most bedrooms offer concealment in the form of a bed and can easily be arranged to provide tactical advantages. Use the following diagram to test yourself.

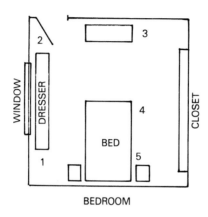

BEDROOM

In position "1" you could be vulnerable to an attack from the window. In position "2" you could be shot through the door, or could be knocked off balance should the assailant force the door into you. Position "3" would put you too close to the entrance, and an assailant might be able to surprise you and take your gun away, as well as be dangerously close to return fire. Position "4" or "5" would provide concealment from an attack coming from either the direction of the door or window, and give you excellent vision to keep both areas covered. Area 5 would be best because you would be farther from the door, but still close enough to be very accurate.

As we have done in the living room and bedroom, you should map all rooms in your home. One of your biggest advantages is you know your home and an assailant doesn't as a rule. Before going into the many other aspects of tactics in the home, the following interview with Lewis Chang, who serves as a Range Master with the Bakersfield Police Department in California provides more insight into self defense tactics for the private citizen.

Q. Could you describe your duties?

A. I am responsible for training police personnel in the use of lethal force. I conduct firearms training to insure they are proficient in the use of firearms, and that they understand the legal and moral aspects relative to the use of lethal force.

Q. Is this just new recruits?

A. No. I also conduct in-service training for all personnel including the reserves.

Q. Do you find it is more effective to have continual training?

A. Yes. Skill with firearms, particularly handguns, is easier to maintain with regularly scheduled training. Officers of our Department must qualify six times a year. This does not include their initial training. Courses of fire are designed with specific objectives in mind such as shoot-don't-shoot situations, running targets, fire and movement, etc. I have found repetition is an important factor in developing proper skills, whereas sporadic efforts are not effective at all.

Q. And for our readers what do you suggest?

A. Practice on a regular basis. For instance, if you took an instructional course such as offered by ISI, upon completion of the course you should have acquired certain skills. Without practice on a regular basis, the skills you worked hard to acquire would deteriorate very rapidly. In fact, if you did not practice for six months after completing your instructional course, you would be lucky to retain 40% of those skills.

Q. So shooting isn't like riding a bicycle?

A. Well, you don't forget how to ride a bicycle, and you probably won't forget how to shoot a gun. But without sufficient practice in shooting, you may not be able to hit what you shoot at, and hitting is what is important.

Q. What about mental conditioning?

A. Mental conditioning is probably one of the least emphasized aspects of survival and very likely the most important. Hypothetical situations should be given thought, and by thinking about these situations, responses can be planned. Then, if a lethal situation should occur, less time would be spent thinking about alternatives, thus giving you more time to act.

Q. What about mental awareness for the average citizen?

A. Awareness for any individual is important to survival. Many life threatening situations can be avoided if you see them ahead of time.

Q. What about training for the citizen?

A. It has been said that in a life and death situation, when there is no time to think, you will react exactly the way you have been trained. Training should be realistic and planned responses to given situations should be practiced. For example, if you come home at night and find an armed intruder, what should you do?

Q. Any tips on tactics?

A. Tactics are essentially mental conditioning. Proper planning prevents poor performance.

Q. We are going to ask a few hypothetical questions. First, let's say John Doe is armed and has a good tactical position on an intruder in his home. He doesn't see a weapon in the hands of the intruder, and he wants to command the intruder to halt and assume an offensive position. What is the best way to give commands?

A. Commands should be given in a forceful manner. They should be brief, simple, and easily understood.

Q. What should John Doe look out for?

A. He should keep his distance. Ideally, there should be at least fifteen feet separating John Doe from the intruder. He should be aware of the intruder's hands. What is in the intruder's hands or arm's reach will hurt you.

Q. How effective are threats and playing head games in this situation as described?

A. Threats may or may not be effective. You should never make a statement you are not prepared to carry out. Engaging in conversations and paying attention to the situation is difficult and may be disastrous. It is extremely difficult to talk and shoot at the same time. John Doe should realize that the intruder didn't expect to confront an armed citizen. However, the time spent engaging in conversation is probably allowing the intruder the time to formulate and execute his plan.

Q. Let's say once again that John Doe is armed, and an intruder has taken his wife hostage.

A. It's impossible to say what course of action is more appropriate. I can give you some choices. First, if John Doe surrenders his firearm, then he is as helpless as his wife. However the possibility exists that the intruder will leave and not harm them. Second, he may leave after John Doe and his wife are dead. Third, if John Doe decides to attempt to shoot the intruder, he may accidentally shoot his wife. Any number of things could occur, and I've only mentioned three or four. The hostage situation is impossible to predict because humans are not predictable.

Q. In closing is there anything you would like to say.

A. Yes. People have the right to self defense. No one wants to take the life of another human being. However, if you have to defend your life at the cost of the life of your assailant, so be it. If you choose to lay down and die, that too is your right. Those who decide to defend themselves, and accept the responsibility and demands involved in being capable to do that, can survive.

LOCATION OF YOUR HANDGUN

All your skills and self defense tactics will be of no use without your firearm. It is imperative your weapon be strategically located in your home for quick access in time of need. It is a good idea to have two weapons in your home, because this will allow you to keep them in different areas. You can not depend or hope, when someone breaks in to your home, that your weapon will always be near you. **It has to be!** If you have only one handgun, you could be in real trouble if an intruder is in between you and where you keep your weapon. You want to be able to quickly grab your gun before an intruder has much time to familiarize himself with your home or possibly notice your presence. If you keep your gun in either a very hard to reach place or somewhere it will take you a moment or two to reach, you place yourself in jeopardy of losing sight of the intruder or having the intruder move to where you are no longer certain of his location. If someone is trying to gain entry into your home, the time you spend trying to get to your weapon could take away some of your defensive advantages.

This would be a good kitchen location.

Ideally, when you are at home, you will always have a weapon near you. If you have only one handgun, then designate a safe area in each room where it can be kept. If you spend most of your time in one room, then make it a habit to keep your weapon in that room. Try to avoid having an area of entry, such as a door, between you and where you keep your gun. An example is the living room. Don't keep your gun on a shelf where it would require you to pass a doorway to get to it.

Your handgun, in the bedroom, should be kept at least one step away from your bed. This is extremely important for everyone's safety! Many of us, when first awakened, are groggy. That step you will take to reach your handgun will give you time to become more alert as well as take in more information. The worst possible place for a gun in your bedroom is under a pillow or hanging from a bedpost or on top of a table within arm's reach of your bed. There are actual cases of people who have fired their weapon while sleeping. If you are or have a member of your household who is a sleep walker, then you must give very careful consideration to this danger. Someone who walks in his sleep is very capable of finding and pulling the trigger of a loaded weapon. Depending on the severity of the condition, you might not be able to safely keep a firearm in your home, at least not where the sleep walker can get to it. This is an area where you should consult a doctor. Only a doctor can advise you on the potential risk, based on the severity of the individual's condition.

Wherever you place your handgun in the bedroom it must not be visible! One of the biggest fears we all have is of waking up in the middle of the night with an intruder standing over us pointing a gun or knife at us. Precautions such as a dog and bedroom door locks can help prevent this from ever happening. Don't invite an intruder to arm himself with your weapon! The ideal hiding place would be to hollow out a book and strap it underneath an end table or mix it in with other books on a shelf. Some other methods are placing an open magazine on top of the gun or some clothes, but when you do this, remember the better you hide your weapon the less likely anyone but you will find it.

The location of your gun in your bedroom is strictly for when you are sleeping in the room. When you are not sleeping, the gun should be with you in whatever area of your home you plan on staying. If you are away from home, it should be stored in a much more secure and hidden fashion. Keep in mind it is your responsibility to secure your gun in a safe and hidden place in such a manner that someone who might burglarize your home would be unlikely to find it. You have a responsibility to the general public to properly secure your weapon. Many of the guns used by criminals were stolen from homes where the owners were negligent in this area. You have a responsibility for your own well being as well. You don't want to return home to find that someone has broken in,

Even in a peaceful setting like this, trouble could strike instantly. Pre-planning is essential.

The homeowner has cleverly concealed his handgun where it can be obtained in the shortest possible time.

In a few moments he is ready to defend himself and his loved one.

found your weapon, and is now threatening you with your own gun. For everyone's safety, secure your handgun where it will not be easily found.

When you are at home, your weapon should be fully loaded. In the high pressure situation of self defense, you can not afford to lose precious time trying to load your weapon. You will need every second to evaluate the situation and to react.

You should keep spare ammunition with your handgun. If you have a semi-automatic, keep a fully loaded spare magazine. With the revolver, you should keep a speed loader or at least a strip loader. Decide in advance how you will carry the spare ammunition. When dressed you will probably have pockets; but when sleeping, this may not be the case. You can't carry the spare ammunition in your hand; because one hand will carry your gun, and the other may carry a flashlight, or you may need both hands for a confrontation. Devise some type of carrying device you can quickly and easily put on. Do not leave your spare ammunition behind. You may find you need it and then it's too late, or you might leave it out in plain sight and now your intruder knows you may be armed. This will effect the element of surprise you need on your side.

Life Without Fear

A home in which only responsible adults live has many more places open as to where you can keep your weapon. There are, however, areas where you don't want to hide your weapon. Drawers are one of the first places criminals look for valuables, especially night stands. Criminals also look in medicine cabinets for drugs and bathrooms in general are not a good idea. There is too much humidity and overall a lack of hiding places. Any place where a criminal would look for valuables is out. Any area which is out of sight but still accessible is where you should keep your weapon.

At times when your handgun is not going to be left unattended, simply laying a newspaper or magazine on top of it will conceal it for instant use. Pictured is the Detonics .45.

If you have young children in your home, where you keep your gun and where and when you keep it loaded will differ. A negligently placed handgun in a home with children, whose parents have not bothered to educate them about the dangers of a handgun, creates a very dangerous situation. Regardless of how secure the location you choose for your weapon, children who are old enough to understand the dangers of traffic and certain household chemicals are old enough to understand the lethal capabilities of a firearm. **As a parent this is your responsibility.** Children are very curious by nature and simply hiding your gun and pretending it does not exist is possibly betting your child's life against his or her ability to find it. It is your duty as a gun owner to teach your children about guns, what they look like, how to properly use them, and illustrate their destructive capabilities. We suggest that you take your children to a target range or other safe area and equip them with the proper safety equipment such as safety glasses and hearing protection. Then place an unopened can of soda pop about ten yards away and have the child watch you fire a round into it. They will see the can explode and how it is torn apart and flattened by the force. You can show them where the bullet entered and exited and point out what could really happen if a person was the recipient of such force. We say **really** because children are conditioned by watching television to believe that a bullet only makes a little hole in the human body; that the good guys never die from being shot. By doing this you will show them vividly that a handgun is not a toy, but a potentially lethal piece of machinery. This can be done without frightening the child; but if it takes fear to make a child respect a gun and make your home a safer place, then it is worth it. If you feel your child is old enough to learn how to fire a handgun, by all means teach him how to shoot. Not only will it teach him to respect the weapon, but shooting can be a sport the entire family can enjoy.

Once you have trained your children, you will still have a problem . . . . your children's friends. Obviously you can not train every acquaintance of your children about safety. As a result, you still have to take precautions about securely hiding your weapon in a safe location. You also can not depend on other adults placing their firearms in a safe place. Discipline your child! You want to make it absolutely clear if they are visiting someone's home, and see a firearm, short or long, **they are to leave that house immediately** and inform you of what happened. We urge you to talk with the adults in that home, in hope that no child will be injured because of their carelessness. Gun safety with children requires some inconvenience. You have to accept this, after all, your life and the lives of your family are well worth whatever added time it takes to make your home a secure and safe place to live.

Whether you are dealing with children or adults you can never depend on the responsibility of others. There are just as many uninformed and immature adults as there are children. Some adults are often little more than big children, especially when they have enjoyed a few social drinks. Under no circumstances do alcohol or drugs and firearms mix. It is still imperative your handgun be accessible, **but only to you!** You never know how foolish a friend might be. We have seen too many adults claim to know everything about safety with firearms even though they have never fired one. Guns are not intended to be party conversation pieces. Don't display or brag about your gun around a crowd of people. We have all seen good friends do things we never expected, and by trusting someone else to handle your gun you are, in a sense, trusting him with your life. Whether loaded or unloaded your handgun is for self defense or recreation and not to be used for party entertainment.

When you leave your home, we strongly advise the use of a good safe. Most of you probably don't own one, and although it is an added expense it is well worth it. Good safes start around $300, and you don't need a very large one if you use it only to store your weapons. There are some very good floor safes available which offer the extra advantage of being hidden from view. Cannon Safe Co. offers excellent safes at reasonable prices. There may seem to be an obvious contradiction here which must be cleared up. Unless your home has been thoroughly cased, the average burglar isn't prepared to open a safe. We do agree a burglar will assume a safe contains valuables and if you have a small portable model, he may take it. That is why we suggest a floor safe, floormount, or a wall safe. If you can't afford a safe and have devised another way to hide your weapon, be sure not to hide the ammunition in the same place. Store your handgun unloaded. An empty detergent box stored with cleaning supplies is one of the least likely places a burglar will look for valuables; also, your garage, attic and basement are areas a thief will not spend much time rummaging through. With common sense and a little imagination you should have no problem finding a secure and safe location for your handgun.

Two very good examples of good use of concealment. An assailant would have a difficult time hitting either one if he was able to fire.

155

THE CONFRONTATION

You are home and asleep and hear your dog barking. You can tell something is wrong, and for a second all you can think about is you're still half asleep. Within another second, however, you fully understand the situation. You wake your wife and tell her to get the kids and hide according to your rehearsed plan for such an event. While in the hiding place, your wife will call the police, tell them someone is breaking into the house, what you look like, and you are armed. The children will be kept quiet. While she has done this, you have taken your handgun and flashlight, and made your way quietly to the hall door with the flashlight off to check for noises which would indicate someone is in the house. The dog has squealed loudly as if it were hurt, but you don't go to the dog's aid. You grimace and hurt inside, but you know you must concern yourself with the family's safety first. Now assuming someone is in the house, you go to the predesignated area which provides cover, and assume a brace position from the frame of your bedroom door with your handgun aimed at the hallway door. You hear the dog barking again, but he sounds like he's outside. You are now certain someone has entered your home. You begin to hear someone come near the steps leading to the hall door. You hear the door handle turn. You are afraid but do not notice, all your concentration is on that hall door. For a second there is silence, then suddenly a loud bang, and the hall door flies open. In a split second you turn your flashlight on just long enough to see that it is not friend or family, and the burst of light has temporarily blinded the intruder. You also see the intruder is armed with his gun pointed in your direction. Without hesitation you fire two shots, and see the intruder's silhouette fall to the ground. You remain where you are, as does your wife and children. You shout "Okay," keep your eyes on the intruder, and wait for the police to arrive. Your wife hears them outside, gets their attention, and throws them keys to your front door. They enter and you put your gun away, but you remain where you are until they tell you it is safe. You have done everything right, and though shaken, have survived.

The sequence we just described took ninety seconds from the time of the initial alarm, the dog barking, until the two shots were fired. There was no time for panic or confusion. There was also no time for indecision. Also, in the next ten minutes, there was no relaxation until the police arrived and determined the intruder was incapacitated, and it was safe for the family. But think to yourself and be honest, how many of you would have immediately gone to the aid of your family pet? Worse, how many of you would have investigated the noise rather than get everyone in a safe position? Probably too many of you.

The family dog in this case provided the alarm and thus the time necessary for the family to ready themselves for an attack. Most dogs will go to the source of any problem. **Never follow the dog.** If you hear the dog squeal from being kicked or injured, do not go to the aid of your pet. As a rule dogs are a little too quick and rugged for an intruder to seriously injure with the exception of a shooting or knifing which you could not reverse by investigating. Again, don't worry about the dog. If you hear the dog barking, get yourself into action. Assume your barricade position. With others in the home, alert them, and have someone call the police.

If you do not have a dog or alarm system, hopefully you will become aware of an intrusion by strange noises soon enough to have time to get into a barricaded position. Under no circumstances should you go outside to investigate noises. With your tactical planning procedures already embedded in your mind, you should know exactly where to go for both safety as well as the most advantageous position in case of a confrontation. From this point, we will assume the circumstances are such that a safe escape is impossible.

The instant you hear any type of alarm you want to get in the quickest and safest position. Whether you must first get your handgun, or already have it with you, as you move through the home make sure the area ahead of you and behind you is clear. Just because the source of the alarm seems to be outside the home does not mean an intruder has not gained entrance. If there are others in the house, they must be kept quiet. You need to be able to hear every sound to determine the source of the problem. It could be a false alarm, and if it is, investigating it will not be of any benefit. There is always the possibility of a dog or wild animal in the garbage, or kids playing a prank. There is also the possibility of it being a noisy friend or family member. The real problem is patience during the waiting period when you simply are not sure if a serious problem exists. If it is friend or family making the noise, you have no reason to find them. They aren't a threat by making noise, just a nuisance. **Stay where you are.** The only exception would be if you heard a cry for help from a known voice. In this case you must proceed with extreme caution. Your approach should be as quiet as possible. Do not go running through the house in a careless manner, forgetting your training. This is an extreme situation. You are forced into investigating. You could find it is a false alarm, or you could find yourself in a hostage situation.

Those of you who take advantage of instituting some type of early warning system will have time to get everyone together and prepare fully for a confrontation. We will now assume you are in the barricaded position, and a presumed intruder is approaching. Remember, in the night or low light situation you should have a flashlight with you. You must always identify the target to be sure that individual does not belong in the home. In all cases you must identify the target and the potential or existence of a lethal threat. Even though you're **sure** someone has broken into your home, you must realize the "intruder" **might** be a neighbor come to help, a family member, the police or even the fire department.

In the low light situation, when you need to use a flashlight, it should be turned "on" and "off" quickly. When you are identifying the target this should be done at a safe distance, and your gun should be aimed at the target. If you can do so safely, request him to identify himself. If you encounter an unidentifiable stranger with a firearm, who will not respond, you must shoot instantly. If you see it is someone you do not know, and do not see a weapon, issue a verbal command to halt. Psychology is important here. You must not sound hesitant or polite. If it turns out to be friend or family, apologies are optional. You must act on the assumption that it is an intruder. Your commands must be brief and forceful. A criminal will not adhere to commands which are not made in this manner.

Once you have made your command to halt, several things may happen. It may turn out to be friend or family, or before you may be a harmless drunk who stumbled into your home. It could be a cat burglar who wants nothing to do with an armed homeowner, or you may have a vicious criminal standing in front of you. As for friend or family it goes without saying the problem is over. In any other case, the cat burglar, the unknown drunk, or the vicious criminal, must all be treated as a potentially lethal threat. It is not up to you to decide someone's intentions or the legitimacy of whatever excuse they provide for wrongfully entering your home. Let the police separate fact from fiction. **You do not want conversation!** You want the intruder to halt, get his hands in full view and assume an offensiveless position, such as hands on head, fingers interlocked.

The individual may react in many ways. Under no circumstances are you to presume anything other than the worst. Proper self defense tactics do not involve predictions or intuition. You must prepare for the worst, and be ready to respond appropriately to any aggressive actions.

If the intruder upon your command turns and runs, do not shoot. You have no reason to fire. No one is a threat with his back turned, fleeing from you. Do not start following the individual for any reason. The intruder might think you are stalking him and are about to kill him, which could lead to a gun battle in which you have no cover or concealment. Also, there could be more than one intruder, and you might find yourself in a trap. Let the intruder escape and wait for police to arrive and clear your home.

Your command might also simply startle the intruder. As long as you do not see a weapon, but can see his hands, reissue your commands. The next move is up to him, and by reissuing your order to halt with fingers interlocked on his head, you are in effect telling him he can comply or die. If he goes for a weapon, or appears to be reaching to an area of his body where a weapon could be kept, you must stop him. You

There are a number of good tactics employed in this scene. Take a separate sheet of paper and write down all the tactical points you see. Check your observations on page 197.

can not wait until he has the opportunity to fire a shot, in spite of how commanding a position you hold. At some point he will do something. It is human nature to react to someone pointing a gun at you, who has total control of the situation. Your cover must be maintained at all times. You never take your eyes off him and you must watch his hands.

When the stalemate ceases, he might not raise his hands, but he also may not take aggressive action. If this occurs, assume he is up to something. If he begins to engage in conversation, tell him to "shut up." Never start conversing with him. If he takes lethal aggressive action, it must be stopped. By continually repeating your commands, eventually the individual will most likely comply. He has tested your determination, and found you will not be tricked.

If there is more than one intruder in the house and you have an intruder under your control, it is critical he be kept completely quiet. If the other intruder advances toward your position, you must be able to hear his approach. You have no choice but to maintain your position, keep total control of the captured intruder, and be ready for any other intruders.

When the intruder is under your control, never take your eyes off him or move from your position. Wait for the police. Do not relax or engage in conversation. It is best for you to keep quiet once you have the intruder where you want him. Even though it appears the worst is over, be ready for any type of aggressive action. If at anytime the situation changes and the intruder takes lethal aggressive action, remember it must be stopped.

In all cases, emotions will be at an extreme of which you might never have experienced before. You must concentrate, however, on maintaining your position and advantage until the police arrive. All this, of course, is under the assumption you or someone else in your home has been able to contact the police. If you are alone and were not able to call the police prior to the confrontation, you have a decision to make in which we can only offer you alternatives. The problem is getting to a phone and call the police. This means leaving your command position and walking with the intruder. Once you leave the command position, you become more vulnerable; and you can be sure a violent criminal will look for the first opportunity to gain control of the situation. Your confidence in your abilities, and your evaluation of the intruder concerning his capabilities will have to be your guide. If you feel you can safely move with the intruder to a phone, you should still proceed with extreme caution. As you move, keep your distance from the intruder. Don't let him walk with his hands to his side, you want his hands behind his head, fingers interlocked. Let him know that you will stop any aggressive action. When you get to a phone, make him lie face down with hands still behind his head. You want his head positioned so he can not see what you are doing. Go to a phone that provides you with the best possible position. When you dial keep your eyes on the intruder. Dial the operator for assistance, rather than rummaging for the phone number through a phone book. When making this decision keep in mind the possibility of other intruders. Don't be foolish and assume you have everything under control. You probably will, but to be safe, always maintain alertness for the possibility, and keep the area behind you clear as you move, or make the phone call. If you do not feel you can safely get to a phone, the only option is to let the intruder escape. If you do this, get to a phone and call the police as soon as it is safe. Then remain in a good barricaded position until the police arrive, and let the police clear your home for you. The main point here is what's in your best interests. Using your common sense, the decision boils down to acting in a manner in which your safety comes first, and apprehension second.

Some of you are probably saying to yourself, "I'll just frisk him, tie him up, and then call the police." We advise against this! Most hardened criminals are very good at disarming tactics. They actually

This is a type of situation that must be avoided. Even though she has the attacker surprised, she has left herself in the open with no cover or concealment and is dangerously close. A swift move could turn the entire situation in favor of the attacker.

161

practice this for recreation while in prison, and they are very good at it. Once you get within an arms length of one of these individuals, your gun can be taken away from you within a fraction of a second. Even police will wait for help before frisking and handcuffing a suspect. The same is true for those of you who decide to clear your home by yourself or investigate strange noises. It is completely idiotic to put your life in jeopardy when you possess good tactical alternatives. **Don't be foolish, stay alive!**

If the circumstances are such that you do have to shoot, and as a result the intruder has been hit and apparently incapacitated, the first thing you must do is control yourself from feeling victorious. Maintain your position and determine where his hands are in relation to the weapon you saw, or the possible areas a weapon might be. You must not run up to him, however well intentioned, to inspect the extent of injuries or to provide first aid. If he's faking, you're dead; if not, unless you are a doctor there is little you can do anyway. Even if you are a doctor, we still feel you should remain where you are until the police arrive, consider your safety before the welfare of someone who has just forced you to defend your life with lethal force.

Regardless of the position of the intruder or the appearance of severe injuries, order him into a defenseless position. Keep in mind the appearance of blood is often deceiving. What looks like a great deal of blood loss to one without medical experience, might not have been enough to render an assailant incapacitated. Even a severely injured assailant can regain enough strength after the initial shock of being shot to fire more shots after lying motionless for several minutes. The best thing to do is remain in your command position until help arrives.

If you must move from your position to phone for help, you must proceed with caution. If a weapon is visible, use only an object such as a coat hanger to get it out of the immediate area of the assailant. Always be careful when handling a gun with which you are not familiar. Some hand made guns will literally go off by gripping the handle. When approaching the assailant, try to do it from an angle in which he can not see you. Be ready for any sudden movements. Keep your gun aimed at the assailant, and be aware of any object near the assailant such as a fireplace poker which could be used against you. **You must stop any aggressive action!** When going to a phone, stay as far away from the intruder as possible. If you must climb over him to get to a phone, keep your eyes on his hands. Do not frisk him. Get around him as quickly as possible. Once you make your phone call, maintain your distance from the assailant. You should do this from cover or concealment. You can never be sure the assailant will not at some point recover enough to attack. You can never let your guard down until the police arrive and clear your home. You can never be too safe, only too sorry.

PREVENTION

Tactics are as much prevention as they are a plan of action for a confrontation. Answering your door carefully is a perfect example of avoiding trouble before it begins. Too many people are very casual about letting strangers into their homes without considering the possibility the desire to gain entrance is not for legitimate reasons. A perfect example is a very successful "con" a team of criminals used. An attractive woman would knock on a door, explain she had car trouble, and requested the use of the home owner's phone to call for help. Most men were quick to oblige, and all who were accommodating were both surprised and disappointed when her two burly companions proceeded to subdue the homeowner, and burglarize the contents of the home. This method is not unusual, and a conman will do anything to enter your home for reasons unknown to you until he achieves entry.

The proper way to answer your door would be keeping it locked and using a device to see who is there. If it is someone you do not know, or are not expecting such as a service technician, do not let him inside. Unless you have a window near the front door which provides you with a full view, you should install a "peephole" with either a pivoting action, or one which has a curved lens providing a full view. Peepholes are inexpensive and easily installed. You don't want to install any type of device which allows large areas to be hidden from view, or which requires the door to be opened a crack. Chain locks, still widely used, can be broken with extreme ease, and provide literally no protection at all. Along with the "peephole," it is a good idea to install a small door to talk through. This would allow you to exchange information without opening your door.

Sometimes you might be expecting someone you do not know such as a service man, or sales person. Most can be trusted, but for peace of mind we feel it is an excellent prevention method to have your handgun with you in a concealable position. This is actually a good habit to get into whenever answering the door. Even though it is legal to carry a handgun with you while in your home, by all means, keep it concealed. You will either unnecessarily alarm an innocent party, or alert a possible assailant that you are armed.

Another area of caution is when you have returned home from work, shopping, or any other activity. It is amazing how many people blindly get out of their car and walk in a home which is being burglarized and are injured or killed needlessly. If only they had developed good awareness habits, most of them would have realized long before they entered the house something was wrong.

When you pull into your driveway take a few seconds and check the immediate area. Is something out of place; is there a car in the driveway or in front of the house which looks suspicious? By being suspicious

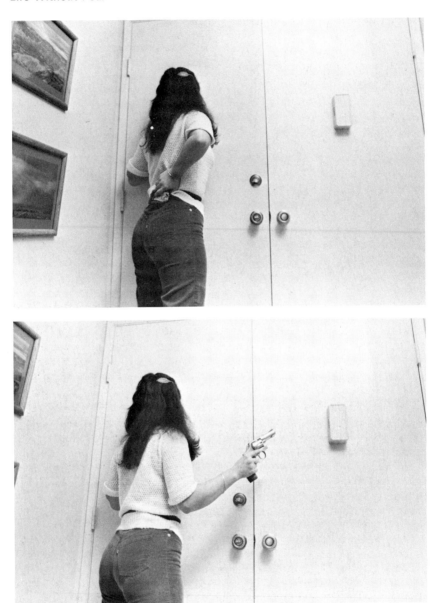

TOP: When answering the door, it's a good idea to have your handgun ready in case you observe danger through your "peep hole." BOTTOM: If danger is present, you are ready immediately. Also, notice the "dead bolt" lock; your front and back doors should both have one.

your common sense should tell you if someone is sitting in a car in front of your house or worse, in your driveway, an alarm should go off in your head! If this happens in your driveway, note the license number, back out of there, and get to a phone and call the police. Let the police ask the individual why he's there; don't take a chance. A car on the street however could be nothing, but always keep track of it until it is gone, and write down the license number if you can obtain it safely.

Before you exit your car look at any possible hiding areas around the immediate area. As you enter your home you should continue to check out your surroundings. Before entering you should also take a look at the windows and doors, being sure everything is the way they were left. If not, and you are convinced someone may be inside, leave and call the police. Your children should be taught these same prevention methods as well.

There are many things you can do to enter your home safely. First, whatever entrance you are most likely to use, keep the area clear of hiding places. Overgrown bushes provide a good hiding place, and create a dangerous situation. For those times when you will be returning home after dark have your exterior lighting on a timing system. Keep a

During your tactical exploration of your home or business, be sure to take into consideration any mirrors or other reflecting objects that could give away your position.

flashlight in your car for walking to the house. Have your high beams on when you pull up in your driveway. When you enter the home, you should have a light switch available as soon as you enter. Keeping a light inside the home either "on," or on an intermittent timer is also advisable.

One of the sad realities of our society today is by dressing fashionable, wearing expensive jewelry, and driving a newer automobile, you instantly become a more likely target for a mugging or assault. A perfect example is a recent situation in which a professional thief working alone boldly picked out a particular supermarket in which a very wealthy clientele shopped. He would pick out a woman who wore the finest in clothing and jewelry. He would then follow the woman home, beat the occupants, and rob them of all their valuables. He was successful for many months. Awareness on the part of most victims could have prevented the situation from effecting them. The man was finally caught because a woman noticed she was being followed and used her car phone to alert police. It was ironic in that, if the criminal had not chosen someone who could afford a car phone, he still might be on the loose today. Obviously, how you dress, the jewelry you wear, and the car you drive, can increase your need to be aware of what is taking place around you.

In general the following are things you should develop a habit of checking when entering your home:

1. Strange vehicle in your driveway.
2. Vehicle in front of your home, or a neighboring home which looks suspicious.
3. Someone wandering around your home, or hiding.
4. A window or door is not in the same condition as when you left.
5. Someone is in your home when no one else is supposed to be there.
6. You have been followed home by someone you do not know.

When we talk to people in our Self Defense training classes about these simple precautions, sometimes someone will comment it sounds like we are promoting paranoia more than anything else. To someone who is careless about such things as awareness and prevention, it might sound that way. If you ask someone who has been a victim, he will tell you he learned the hard way. The bottom line is considering the few seconds it takes for prevention, coupled with the fact it simply becomes a healthy habit quite quickly; it no longer sounds paranoid, it simply makes sense. If there is a problem, you want to become aware of it early and leave. What you do not want is to become part of the problem, and suffer injury or death from carelessness.

Prevention is also important when you are in your home. Most of us have somewhat regular schedules, and we know when someone is supposed to come in or out. Regardless, including children, when any family member or friend enters your home, make it a house rule for the persons entering to give a yell and identify themselves. There is nothing worse than failing to institute this simple prevention measure, and have a criminal enter your home unknown to you until it is too late. With daytime burglaries on the increase, don't make this mistake. People who enter your home should have a key, allowing you to keep all doors locked. Doors should never be left unlocked for the convenience of friends or family members. If your friend is trusted enough to simply enter your home without knocking, that friend can be trusted with a key. If a child is old enough to enter and exit your home unescorted, the child is old enough to have a key. Many people hide keys; it really isn't a bad idea, especially with children, **but hide it!** The under-the-welcome-mat, or top shelf of an unlocked garage is inviting trouble. If you must keep a key hidden, do it wisely and cleverly.

We have discussed the location of your handgun previously, but we want to make it clear from the standpoint of prevention, that your handgun will be of little help if it is not accessible, or you are not sure where it is located. In the case of a family, or a roommate situation where two people share the same handgun, keep each other advised as to its location. Ideally you want your gun kept as near to you as possible when home. For the housewife, if you are home alone, and know you will be in one room for any length of time, keep it with you if possible. The same holds true for men as well. If the children are home, from a safety standpoint, wherever you keep it, make sure it is not accessible to any children.

We would like to pay special attention to those of you who might at sometime for some reason believe your life is in danger. You might have been threatened, received abusive phone calls, been a witness to a serious crime, have had a dispute because of a personal relationship, or other situations in which someone has lethally threatened you in some manner. We strongly believe you should have your handgun with you at all times while this situation persists. If someone has verbally threatened you, do not brush it off. First let the police know a threat has been made. Second, think, if someone is angry or crazy enough to threaten to take your life and commit the worst of all crimes, that individual just might be sick enough, or criminal enough to follow through on the threat. Protect yourself and be especially aware in this situation. Keep the police notified of any continuing threats, and do not engage in an exchange of threats with the individual threatening you. Don't tell him you are armed, don't tell the individual anything. From a tactical standpoint this would be the worst thing you could do.

MENTAL PREPARATION

The mental preparation involved in surviving a violent attack is a daily exercise. As a rule, there is no advance warning which allows the intended victim to give careful consideration to the necessary steps he will take to counter an attack. In many cases, an individual became a victim when it could have been avoided. As we have stated, criminals prefer an easy mark. In the same vein, the honest citizen can prevent a problem before it begins through awareness. You have to see things as they could be rather than as they appear on the surface.

For instance, a man or a woman dressed neatly rings your doorbell and asks to enter your home to discuss a great deal which could be to your advantage. You say to yourself: "He or she is dressed nicely and talks well, and it certainly sounds like something I'm interested in," so you let him inside. If you saw things as they could be, you would not let a stranger into your home. You would instead ask him to leave his brochure, and say you will call him and set up a more convenient time, tactfully avoiding a possibly serious problem. To let this person inside your home based on trust and appearances is not practicing awareness but allowing others to rule your actions. Being careful is not the same as being rude.

Every person who rings your doorbell is not a vicious murderer. Every person who says hello to you on the street is not planning on putting a knife in your back. Awareness and paranoia are not synonymous. Awareness is simply paying attention to your surroundings and playing it safe. Awareness means denying a person a chance to put you in a vulnerable position. A perfect example of awareness is the person who locks his car doors and always checks the interior of the car when he returns to make sure no one has gained entry. A foolish person will assume that because the car was locked it's safe to get in without checking. Awareness tells you it is better to walk in a lighted area at night than in a dark alley, even though it is quicker. If someone seems to be following you, take evasive actions such as picking up your pace, crossing the street, or if you are in your car, driving in an evasive manner not only to lose the car following you but to determine if you are indeed being followed. Even if you are wrong about your impression, it's better to feel a little foolish than to become an easy target.

Common sense is your guide. Think about what you're doing and about what you're going to be doing. If you are going to walk across a parking lot to your car, have your keys out and ready. Common sense also includes intuition. If you have uncomfortable feelings about a situation or a person around you, leave! Don't talk yourself out of being concerned. You will never be able to talk yourself out of regretting a big mistake. The lack of exercising common sense gets more people into trouble than anything else. As long as you approach what you are doing with common sense, you will avoid many serious situations and enjoy a more secure life.

Awareness and common sense, although effective preventative measures, won't always keep us out of trouble. When trouble strikes, it usually STRIKES instantly. Accept the fact you may very well have to make a split second decision. How many times have we heard victims recount an incident and the use of the expression "but it all happened so fast?" Trouble can happen unnervingly fast, and your reaction must be just as fast. There will be no time to leisurely evaluate the situation. Immediate reactions to a life threatening situation are not automatic for most of us. We all have a natural instinct to survive; we were born with it. This instinct is the foundation you will use to develop the ability to react automatically and immediately to a threatening situation.

In our somewhat civilized society many of us have lost our ability to quickly draw on this instinct, and we must consciously redevelop this ability. The biggest stumbling block you may face is disbelief. We can not understand why anyone would want to harm another person; therefore, we react with disbelief, much the way we react to the news of a death. You can develop your natural instinct through practice. Visualize taking a walk when suddenly an armed person jumps out at you from behind a tree, think about what you would do and then practice your actual reactions with a friend.

A clarification must be made here. Too many people think that drawing on the instinct to survive means going half crazy, biting, clawing, and behaving like a rabid animal. This book is designed to teach you a variety of tactics and skills you can draw on in different situations. You will not find it easy to utilize if you become a raving maniac. What you should strive for is a reaction of calculated aggressiveness. It is an efficient reaction because you will draw on knowledge and this knowledge will give you the coolness to apply it properly. Calculated aggressiveness is an absolute resolution that you will not withdraw or hesitate while defending yourself until the attacker has escaped or been stopped. Your commitment to survival means you do not concern yourself with the injury you may inflict on any individual who has violently attacked you until this individual is no longer a lethal threat.

Many people who teach self defense speak in terms of coolness, "keeping your wits about you." Coolness is not a part of the mental skills, it is simply a by-product. You will do the right things and survive if you prepare yourself to do them. They will become second nature because you worked at it. They will not come to you when you need them the most just because you calmly and coolly stared death in the face. On television we see guys who have just gone through one of their weekly life and death struggles, crack a joke the second it was over, and act like it was no big deal. Well, that isn't the real world. Without skills, without preparation, it won't matter how brave and cool you think you are, you can still end up a big loser.

Most people, who read this book, who do find themselves in a life or death situation will probably find they didn't feel very calm, but because of their practice and determination to survive, they did what they had to do to stay alive. They may be told they handled themselves and the situation very calmly, though they might have felt anything but calm. They will find they were so busy concentrating on the situation and drawing on their knowledge and skills they didn't think about their nervousness or fears until it was all over.

TACTICAL EMPLOYMENT OF BASIC STYLES AND TECHNIQUES

When practicing, you will learn first hand the advantages and limitations of the different styles of shooting. Whenever possible you should use the techniques which will provide you with the optimum in speed and accuracy. You will achieve this by applying the fundamentals we discussed in the chapter on basic styles and techniques. For instance you will be using the two handed grip, be in a concealed position, and aim fire whenever time allows. In a low light situation without a flashlight, you will likely have to point fire. In the case of a total surprise attack, you might have to use instinct shooting. When shooting from cover or concealment, you should be able to utilize the brace shooting technique. If you have apprehended an intruder, you will not be able to watch the assailant and focus on the front sight at the same time. In this case, you will be depending on point firing should the intruder take sudden aggressive action. As we have stated, in a confrontation you will react and will not have excessive time to think. The shooting technique you use during a confrontation will be determined by your training as well as common sense. There are, however, certain techniques which will differ from your routine practice when in a real self defense situation.

RELOADING UNDER FIRE

The chances of having to reload under fire during a self defense situation are small, but not small enough to ignore this important skill. Speed is extremely important, and you must practice so you can reload without looking at your handgun. You also can't be concerned with where you drop your spent cartridges or magazine as you probably do at a practice range. Recently a highway patrol officer was killed in a shooting, and six empty cartridges were found in his pocket. For some reason, probably because he never practiced for the possibility of reloading under fire, he wasted precious time putting his spent cartridges in his pocket. The problem is while at the range you will ordinarily not let your cartridges or magazines fall to the ground, but part of your practice must include doing this, so if the situation does arise, you will not waste any time.

Should you have to reload, the speed at which you can accomplish this will increase your chances of survival. **No one is going to wait for you to reload.** While you reload, three things may happen. The assailant may change positions (more than likely it will be a better position for him), he may rush you, or he may decide to take aim and get off a good shot. For these reasons it should be obvious why you must learn to reload without looking at your gun, and you must be able to keep your eyes on the assailant. Also, the ideal situation would be to reload before you are fully out of ammunition. It is difficult to count shots, but if for any reason there is a pause in shooting, and you have expelled more than four shots in a revolver, or four to five in a semi-automatic with a capacity of eight rounds, take the opportunity to reload. If you are using a revolver, you should have a speed loader. When you reload, expel all cartridges, spent and live, and reload. If you are using a strip loader, you can reload two or three rounds without expelling any live cartridges, but you will have to take your eyes off the assailant. With the semi-automatic, expel the spent magazine, and replace it with a new one.

Whenever you reload, try to do it behind cover or concealment. If this is not possible, it is far better to reload on the move, rather than be a stationary target and a "sitting duck." You must practice reloading on the move in preparation for such a situation.

In general, the most important factor is speed when reloading. You should practice so no motions are wasted. Also, let the spent cases or magazine drop to the ground. Practice this by feel and also by sight, so you will be able to reload quickly no matter what the situation.

NIGHT SHOOTING

We must stress the importance of identifying the target in a night shooting situation. Also, the night time situation is the one in which most people seem intent on investigating noises, and hunting down a possible intruder. As we have stated previously, this should seldom be done. Once you have your handgun and flashlight, get into a barricaded position behind cover or concealment and prepare to identify the target. You should never shoot at anyone or anything unless you are sure of what you are shooting. Just because you heard the window break, or heard voices you did not recognize, and are sure there are intruders in the house does not mean you start shooting at shadows or noises. What if it turns out to be a family member or policemen, possibly even a neighbor who saw the commotion and tried to help. Everyone should have a high powered flashlight kept with his gun at night. If you don't have one or the flashlight doesn't work, you can't be turning a light "on" without giving away your position and cover, unless it is switch operated light which can be turned on from a safe position. In most

In the low light or night shooting situation, you will most likely be using the point firing technique. Target identification and justification to shoot must be made before firing, therefore, stay in your barricaded position and keep the element of surprise on your side.

homes you might have no choice but to wait the precious seconds, possibly minutes it might take your eyes to adjust to the lack of light. With the exception of a cave, most homes will still have enough light at night for you to see once your eyes have adjusted. The best thing is to avoid this problem and invest in a good flashlight.

The techniques we discussed in our chapter on Basic Styles and Techniques apply to all night shooting situations. We do want to stress the importance of daytime practice as it relates to night shooting, and night practice when possible to build your night shooting skills.

Remember in low light situations there are more hiding places for you and an intruder. Move with extreme caution when going to your barricade position. Always think of possible outside light sources such as light from a street lamp or neighbor's home. A shadow will give away your position to an intruder. If you must turn a light on, do it from concealment or cover and use your weak hand. All the tactics discussed in this chapter apply to night shooting. You will simply have to be more patient and controlled in this situation.

USING THE FLASHLIGHT

When you turn on your flashlight, you have to expect an intruder might shoot at the light. Therefore, we highly recommend the technique in which you hold the flashlight in your weak hand out and away from your body as far as possible. If you are looking around a corner, don't hold it next to your head. It is far safer to hold it high over your head. Another way to do this from a corner is to place it on the ground about six inches to a foot from the corner and turn it "on". With a powerful flashlight this will illuminate a large area, and also enable you to shoot with both hands.

The flashlight must always be used with the lamp part out in front of your body. If you have the lamp too close to your body, your body could be illuminated by your own light. If for some reason you must walk with the flashlight, or scan an area from a concealed position, do not keep the light on continuously. The intruder will quickly learn exactly where you are located. Turn the light on, check the immediate area and then turn it off. Whenever you must move with the flashlight, move as soon as

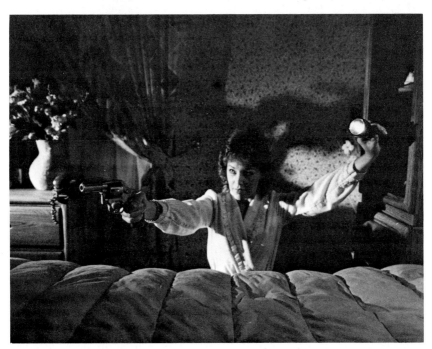

This is the flashlight technique we recommend. By keeping the light to your side and ahead of your body, an assailant won't know your exact position. For purposes of illustration, she is upright. You should practice with only your eyes, gun and flashlight visible.

173

you are sure the area is clear, and you have turned the light off. Do not walk around with the light on, or be using it without cover or conceal-ment. You should try to move as much as possible without turning the light "on". You should know your home, and only use the flashlight to identify the target. A powerful flashlight when shined in the eyes of an intruder will temporarily disorient and blind him. It is very wise to invest in not only a reliable flashlight, but also one which is powerful enough to provide you with this added advantage.

A powerful flashlight will temporarily blind and disorient an intruder, giving you precious time to identify and react.

THE PEEK TECHNIQUE

In certain situations, you will have no choice but to go around a corner in your home, or possibly on the street. If you casually move around a corner, you become easy prey for someone who might be waiting for you. Just looking around a corner can be very dangerous if it isn't done properly. When you do peek around the corner you must expose only the eye you are looking with, and as little of the head as possible. Your shoulder, arms, and legs should not be visible to someone around the corner. When you "peek," it is just that, a very quick peek at a specific area. If you must look again, you will be "peeking" from a different position. For example, the first time you looked around the corner your head would be at a normal heighth, the second time you would be at center or floor level. The object is to have your head in a different position whenever you look. If you keep popping your head out at the same position, you make yourself a very predictable target.

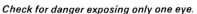

Check for danger exposing only one eye.   *If you must defend your life, fire from a different level.*

Should you see an intruder when you peek, it would not be wise to shoot. You will not be prepared from the standpoint of your positioning. The peek method is for the purpose of identifying the target or clearing an area. Should you identify a target as a lethal threat, you would shoot from a position different from where you peeked the first time. This method is also good to use from cover or concealment, trees if you're outside, a car, etc. The main thing is to make it quick so if the assailant does shoot, you are back out of the line of fire in time.

CARRYING CONCEALED

If you are someone who needs to carry a handgun, there is no need to tell you to be aware, you already must have accepted this fact. Unfortunately there are some irresponsible people in the world who aren't dishonest, but rather simply a dangerous mix of bravado and stupidity. These are the people who whenever someone on the street harasses them a little, or do something they don't particularly like, they pull out their gun and play "Dirty Harry." Not only is this illegal, but it is tactically dangerous as well. First, you've lost the element of surprise. Second, when you point a gun at anyone who has not displayed lethal force, you have just escalated and become part of a criminal activity. Your gun should never be displayed unless lethal force exists and you intend to fire. Self defense does not include using a handgun for the purpose of threatening someone who irritated you. In carrying a concealed weapon, you have accepted a tremendous amount of responsibility. You not only have a responsibility to yourself, but to innocent parties who may be dangerously near, when you display your weapon. If you are harassed, **bite your tongue!** Do everything you can to avoid a situation which could escalate into something more serious.

In any situation where you feel there is a possibility of danger, or there is obvious danger, have your hands in position in case you do have to draw. Also look for anything in your immediate area which might provide cover or concealment. If a lethal confrontation does occur, and you have the time, it would be better to shoot from cover or concealment, or shoot and immediately move rather than be a stationary target. If not, stand your ground and defend your life without hesitation.

What direction you move to for cover or concealment is important. Do not be afraid to give ground if it is going to be advantageous. The main thing you want to do is get out of the line of fire, and into a position which will enable you to shoot the assailant, stopping the attack. It is far better to think while on the move as to where to go, than stand stationary and be an easy target. Movement alone will help, especially when you are up against an attack from a handgun. When you can move it is best to move low to the ground in a zig-zag pattern. Rolling would only be advisable if cover is close to your position. Returning fire while moving to cover usually will do little but provide ineffective distraction. As a rule, you will miss when shooting on the move. You can't aim fire and you would be lucky to point fire. More than likely you would be instinct shooting from a very unstable position; and in missing, you would waste ammunition and possibly endanger innocent people.

In any situation, you must be prepared for possibly more than one attacker. You never turn your back to an assailant, and you never shoot to disarm. If a shooting does take place, you must be prepared for the possibility that an injured assailant may recover sufficiently to fire again. You must keep in mind you are armed, and that citizens and police might not know you're the good guy or the bad guy. They might only see someone has been shot, and you have a gun in your hand. When the police arrive, if your gun is in your hand, don't move a muscle except to drop the weapon and comply with their demands. There will be plenty of time for you to explain who you are, and while you are armed is not the time. If an assailant attempts to flee, don't shoot. You are rarely justified in doing this from a legal standpoint, and we strongly advise against it. Keep in mind the basic rules of Tactics. Whether in your home or on the street, your only concern is surviving. If you carry a concealed weapon, you must be level headed at all times and never let anything but a lethal threat prompt you to use the lethal force you possess.

SHOOTING A MOVING TARGET

To shoot a moving target you would hold on the front of the assailant, the front being the side which is forward and closest to the direction the individual is moving. Your sight picture will move with the target. When you fire, the gun must continue to move with the target. If you stop when you fire, you will most likely miss behind the target. Also, if you hit the assailant and he drops, you are in perfect position for further shots if necessary. If you miss, you are still moving with the target and ready to continue firing more shots rapidly. This is probably the single most difficult skill to develop. With sound fundamentals and practice, you can become quite proficient.

SHOOTING MULTIPLE ASSAILANTS

This is a situation in which you will have two or more attackers posing a threat. This is an extreme situation, but it could happen. It is more common in a street encounter, but could happen in your home as well. This situation will require you to draw on all your skills in order to survive. You can only shoot one at a time, but which one you choose is of critical importance.

The first thing you must do is identify which assailant presents the most immediate danger. For instance, if assailant **A** is a distance of ten feet and has a knife, and assailant **B** is ten feet away and has a handgun, the assailant with the handgun would be stopped first. If assailant **A** were only two feet away, then he would be shot first, as at that range he is the most immediate threat. The reason would be at such a close range assailant **A** could take your gun from you leaving you defenseless against further attack or use your gun against you. If you had a third assailant **C** standing at a 20 foot distance with a shotgun, he would be stopped first providing that assailant **A** or **B** armed with a knife was not close enough to be a more immediate threat. This decision has to be made in a split second. Practicing this on a combat range is extremely valuable.

Once you make the decision of whom to stop first, all your attention must be on that target. If there are only two, fire two shots at the main threat first, and then two rounds at the secondary threat. If there are three or more, you will have to fire one shot at each. You would continue to fire at those who continued to be a lethal threat as long as possible and then reload if necessary. If there are so many that you might run out of rounds, you will probably have to depend on single shots stopping at least one or more of the assailants. If overpowering odds are present, your only hope would be to fire one shot at each assailant and flee the area as soon as possible. If you can't escape, you will have to stop any assailants who continue to be a lethal threat even if it means reloading under fire. Should for some reason, you drop one assailant, and the others decide to abandon the attack, you can not legally shoot the others. Your emotions will be at a peak in this situation and it is difficult for us to tell you exactly how to determine the attack has been abandoned. If a firearm is out and moved at all in your direction, it should be considered a lethal threat and must be stopped. If the assailants have dropped their weapons and run, or have their hands raised, you should not shoot. However, in this situation fractions of a second will be involved in going from one target to another, and you have to make a split second judgement. You can't afford to wait to see whether or not the attack will be abandoned. You have to make a common sense decision as to continued lethal threat and react accordingly.

In a home environment, if cover is available you will be able to position yourself enabling you to control a wider area. In your tactical mapping, do mock exercises in which you make sure your designated areas provide you with enough room to cover all possible angles of fire. If you find you can not do this, you should re-evaluate your designated area so it provides you with the needed wide range of fire.

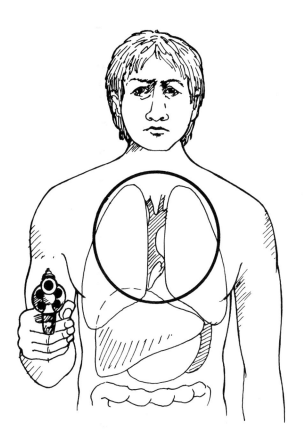

TARGET ACQUISITION

As we have stated when you must shoot, you do so to stop any aggressive lethal action being taken against you. You do not shoot to wound, disarm, or scare an attacker. In most self defense situations you will be shooting the **center mass** as illustrated. By shooting at the center of the "vital zone" of the attacker illustrated with two quick accurate shots, the percentages are greatly in your favor that this will stop the attack. First, your target will be an area composed of vital organs. With the larger caliber guns and proper ammunition, a wound to this area will more than likely cause the assailant to go into shock even if it does not strike the heart or a main artery. When hit with such force, an assailant's body will physiologically react in such a way as to likely render the individual incapable of continuing the attack. However, one shot is often not enough, which is why we suggest two quick, accurate shots. The second wound in most cases will ensure the assailant's body will go into shock. It now has two wounds which are sending messages throughout the body, and more than likely either acute blood loss or disruption of the nervous system will render the assailant incapacitated. The center mass area as a target, and the concept of two shots, gives you the highest percentage of stopping an attack immediately.

Shooting at the head obviously would cause the most immediate and severe damage, if you can hit it. It is a much smaller target than the chest, and also is more likely to be moving in some direction. It would only be advisable to shoot for the head if shots to the center mass appear ineffective, and you suspect the assailant is wearing body armor of some type. If you must shoot for the head, you ideally would aim for the center of the head just above the nose.

When you are in a situation in which you are at the point of aiming at your target, you should aim directly at the center of his body, at about the level of his armpit. Again, when you do shoot, it should be two quick accurate shots. Never shoot one shot and wait to see what happens unless there is more than one assailant. After the two shots have been fired, you must be ready to repeat this action as long as the assailant continues to be a lethal threat. Remember, regardless of how seriously it appears you have injured an attacker, never relax, or approach the downed assailant. When practicing you should use silhouettes whenever possible, so proper target acquisition becomes instinctual.

TACTICS REVIEWED

As you have seen, tactics for the private citizen are a combination of many factors such as prevention, mental preparation, and applying learned shooting skills. Everything we discussed in this chapter is extremely important to your survival. It is suggested from time to time, you review this section. We believe by just reviewing material of this type, it will enhance your chance of surviving a lethal attack. It is unlikely you'll have the ability to fully retain what you have just read the first time through; this is just because there are so many things you have probably never thought about before. And, as we have said many times, should you be involved in a self defense situation, **there will be no time to wonder what to do, you must react quickly.**

CHAPTER 8

RECOMMENDED EQUIPMENT

GUNS

The best gun for self defense in the home or concealed carry will vary according to the individual and the situation. Hand size, willingness to practice, concealability and budget are all factors. There are many different handguns available which are excellent for self defense. At times it will seem confusing when faced with these different choices. We will try to help narrow the choices by giving you some basic information about certain recommended guns. The final decision is yours, but after reading this chapter and going to the range to try out the guns that seem best for you, the purchase should be a bit easier. Most target ranges do rent guns and in addition you may have a friend who is knowledgeable about guns and would be happy to help you make a choice. Expert advice is especially important if you decide to buy a used gun. We will describe the guns we feel are best for self defense, what factors to consider and which modifications may be needed to help you narrow down your choices. There are two basic types of handguns, the revolver, and the semi-automatic which we will refer to as the pistol.

There are many different size revolvers available but just any gun will not do. The stopping power of a gun is a critical life saving factor. Therefore, we recommend a minimum size of .38 Special Caliber in the revolver and 9mm in the pistol. There are three basic frame sizes to consider for the revolver, small, medium and large. Small frame revolvers generally have short barrels. Two inches is most common with some available up to three inches. These handguns are commonly referred to as "snubnose" models because of their short barrel length. They offer maximum concealability. The medium frame revolvers are generally the .38 Special and the .357 Magnum. The large frame revolvers are generally the .41 Magnum, .44 Magnum, .44 Special, .45 Colt and .45 Auto Rim. The size of your hand will be an important factor when choosing the frame size of the revolver.

Semi-automatic pistols are a choice for those who are willing to spend more time familiarizing themselves with their weapon. They require more time because most of their mechanical functions are not external, whereas the revolver's are externally visible and you can see exactly what is happening as you pull the trigger. Pistols, however, have an easier trigger pull because the pressure needed to pull the trigger is as low as three and one half to four pounds whereas the pressure is eight to ten pounds for the revolver. The revolver, which takes longer to load, has a capacity of five to six rounds. The pistol magazines have a capacity of six to eighteen rounds and as a result you have more fire power. As far as dependability, the double action revolver and the pistol are basically equal. Right out of the box from the manufacturer the revolver is usually somewhat more reliable, although it should be tested. There are many times in which the semi-automatic must be modified to accommodate the type of ammunition the owner wishes to use. This can affect the overall cost of the weapon, however, you will have to practice with any weapon you purchase to not only assure its reliability but to become efficient in its use. This brings up a serious situation. If you are one of those people, or you know someone, who went out and purchased any kind of gun and never used it, thinking if the time ever came you'd be able to use it properly, you had better make a decision. **get rid of the gun or resign yourself to learning how to use it!** Too many people have learned the hard way that it is far more dangerous to own a gun you don't know either how to shoot properly or whether or not it's in good working order, than it is to be unarmed.

Before you get the idea that the manufacturers are purposely making semi-automatic pistols in need of repairs before they can be used, we better explain. When the semi-automatic comes from the factory it is set up to use ball ammunition, but if you want to use ammunition that has more stopping power, the pistol will likely need inexpensive modification.

For most people, we feel the best choice for a handgun for home protection is a medium frame, four inch barrel, .38 Special or .357 Magnum caliber. By choosing the .357 Magnum, you have the advantage of being able to practice with the less expensive .38 Special load and for home self defense you can keep the .357 Magnum load which has more stopping power. If you have large hands and are fairly strong, you may want the large frame .44 Special or the .44 Magnum with a four inch barrel.

A basic rule of thumb is the larger the caliber you can effectively handle the more stopping power you will have. We have mentioned stopping power quite a bit which is why we haven't mentioned derringers, .22 calibers or the .25 ACP. They are not reliable unless you think you could shoot a moving target between the eyes, and they have relatively low stopping power. You could shoot a man square in the head with a .22 or .25 and it might not stop him, and it's possible it could ricochet off his skull. Even with the guns we recommend no one is going to be lifted off his feet and sent flying through the air like you see on television. Stopping power is very critical and its purpose is to stop the criminal immediately. We do not recommend a semi-automatic pistol under the 9 mm caliber nor do we recommend a single action revolver. The single action revolver is slow to reload and requires you to manually cock the hammer and then pull the trigger as compared with the double action revolver where the hammer is cocked automatically when you pull the trigger.

The purchase of a handgun represents a substantial investment. By choosing one of the models we have tested and recommended, you will be purchasing a product suitable for self-defense.

RECOMMENDED MODELS

** **Auto-Ordnance:**
.45 ACP, 8 round capacity, 5 inch barrel, fixed sights, 39 ounces, blue finish. It is a well made, budget priced, big bore semi-automatic. Also available in 9mm.

* **Charter Arms Undercover:**
.38 Special, 2 inch barrel, 5 or 6 shot capacity, blue finish or stainless steel, fixed sights. Available with de-horned hammer and rubber grips.

* **Charter Arms Bulldog:**
.44 Special, 5 round capacity, fixed sights, 3 inch barrel, 19 ounces, blue finish or stainless steel, excellent concealable large bore revolver. Available with de-horned hammer and rubber grips.

* **Colt Agent and Detective Special:**
.38 Special, 6 shot capacity, 2 inch barrel, fixed sights, has blued steel frame. Agent is lightweight alloy frame with Parkerized finish.

** **Colt Trooper Mk V:**
.357 Magnum, 6 shot capacity, adjustable sights, 4 inch barrel, shrouded ejector rod, finish available in blue, nickel, or Coltguard.

** **Colt Python:**
Top of the line .357 Magnum revolver, ventilated rib with adjustable sights, extremely heavy duty, available in 2½ or 4 inch barrels, with blue, nickel, or Coltguard finishes, as well as stainless steel in the 4 inch barrel only.

* **Colt Lightweight Commander:**
.45 ACP, eight round capacity, 4½ inch barrel, overall length of 8 inches, weighs 27 ounces, blue finish, alloy frame.

** **Colt Combat Commander:**
9mm or .45 ACP, steel frame version of Lightweight Commander.

** **Colt Government Model:**
45 ACP, eight round capacity. 9 MM or 38 Super 10 round capacity. Blue finish, high quality big bore semi automatic. Needs basic alterations (see modifications, chapter 9) to reach full potential.

** **Colt Combat Government Model:**
.45 ACP, 8 round, high visibility fixed sights, improved ejection port, blue finish, refined version of the Government Model.

Colt "Python" 357 Magnum

Randall Service Model

* Detonics:
.45 ACP, 7 round capacity, 3½ inch barrel, stainless steel, fixed sights, a very compact .45 with an overall length of only 6¾ inches.

* Heckler and Koch:
P-7 Semi-automatic, 9 round capacity, squeeze cock, highly concealable, good accuracy, excellent trigger pull and simple operation.

** Heckler and Koch:
P9S double action, semi-automatic .45 ACP, 8 round capacity or 9MM 10 round capacity, double action, fixed sights.

** Randall Service Model:
.45 ACP 8 round capacity — 5 in barrel. 38 ounces Stainless Steel throughout — comes with hi-visibility fixed sights, lowered ejection port, long trigger, wide grip safety, extended safety and beveled mag well. This is the only .45 that comes from the factory properly modified for self defense. Also available in 9 MM or with adjustable sights.

** Randall Raider:
4½" barrel, overall length of 8 inches, shorter version of the service model .45 ACP or 9MM.

* Randall "Lemay":
Compact model that has a shorter barrel slide and butt. Excellent concealed carry high power automatic. .45 ACP.

** Smith & Wesson:
Model 38 Bodyguard Airweight 38 spl. 5 shot capacity —2" barrel.

** Smith & Wesson:
Model 37 Chief Special, airweight, exposed hammer version of the Bodyguard.

** Smith & Wesson:
Model 65 stainless, Model 13 Blue Steel .357 Military and Police 4" Heavy barrel, fixed sights. One of the best multi-purpose revolvers available.

** Smith & Wesson:
Model 686 Stainless, 586 Blue Steel, Distinguished Combat Magnum .357 Premium grade gun with adjustable sights.

** Smith & Wesson:
Model 469 Blue steel, lightweight 9MM 12 shot fixed sights semi-automatic.

** Smith & Wesson:
Model 659 stainless steel, Model 459 Blue steel 9MM 14 shot semi-automatic, adjustable sights.

** Sturm Ruger Security Six:
.357 Magnum, 6 round capacity, 2¾ or 4 inch barrel, weighs 33½ ounces. The rear sights are completely adjustable with partridge type front sight and is available in blue finish or stainless steel. A very well built revolver and features a one piece frame.

** Sturm Ruger Speed Six:
.357 Magnum, basically the same as the Ruger Security Six, but with fixed sights, round butt, and 2¾ or 4 inch barrel. This model is an excellent choice for smaller hands. Available in blue finish or stainless steel.

** Sturm Ruger Police Service Six:
.357 Magnum, 6 round capacity, 2¾ or 4 inch heavy barrel also built on the **Security Six** frame. It features fixed sights and square butt. It is built for a rough service revolver and the heavy barrel gives it excellent balance. Available in blue finish or stainless steel.

---

* Best suited where maximum concealability is needed.
** Good choice for home defense, range practice or where maximum concealability is not a necessity.

Detonics 45 ACP

Smith & Wesson "Bodyguard"

BUYING NEW OR USED HANDGUNS

As in any major purchase, you should shop around to compare prices. When you find the gun and best price, and are ready to make your purchase, you should carefully inspect it. If it is new, there should be no scratches on it or wear marks from it being taken in and out of a holster. If you see this, possibly it was a demo or it might simply have been a used gun being sold as new by honest mistake or intentionally for profit. This is rare, but it is better to be safe than to have someone take advantage of you. On the revolver, make sure the cylinder works smoothly. Work the trigger, and carefully get a feel as the cylinder turns, to be sure it is synchronized. Sometimes new guns will get through a quality control department, and the timing will not be right on one or more of the cylinders, so be sure to check all of them. On the semi-automatic, check the slide action and trigger pull to make sure it is not set up too stiff. Like all other products, follow warranty instructions, and have it serviced at an authorized factory service center. **Remember,** whenever you are checking out a handgun, follow all safety procedures.

When buying a used gun you will probably not enjoy substantial savings. The handgun is not a terribly complicated piece of machinery, and therefore, has a long life and rarely needs any major repairs. In some states, depending on gun laws and the waiting period, a used gun could actually be more expensive than a comparable new one, so check both out. If you buy from a private party, check the same way you would on a new gun with both the revolver and semi-automatic. If possible, ask if you could go with the owner to a range and try it out. The only major problem you could find is if it has a cracked frame. This is rough for the novice to check, especially on the semi-automatic, but it can be detected. If you want to be sure, take along a friend who knows something about guns. If not, and the owner assures you the gun is in working order, let him put it in writing. Then if it isn't, you can return the weapon within a reasonable period of time and get your money back. You should also make sure, depending on your local laws, that you are buying a legally registered gun to avoid a potential problem in register-ing it. Like buying all goods from private parties, get everything in writing and signed! It could save you a lot of aggravation, and after all, anyone who makes a verbal promise, will write it down if it is legitimate.

AMMUNITION

There are many misconceptions when it comes to deciding what ammunition and gun are best. All handguns do have the capability to kill or seriously injure an individual. The problem is how soon and how well will they neutralize an assailant. Every fraction of a second counts in a self defense situation and it is critical that you realize that the longer it takes for you to stop an attack, the more possible it is for you to be injured or killed in a confrontation.

In our section on recommended guns, you will notice that there are no guns below a .38 caliber recommended. Guns such as the .22, .25, .32 and the .380 are not acceptable for self defense purposes because they don't provide adequate stopping power. When we speak of stopping power, we mean just that. Stopping an attacker does not necessarily mean killing but only to inflict an assailant with a shot, or a series of shots, which will traumatize the attacker to the point where he will be totally incapacitated and unable to continue an attack of any type. You should always shoot to stop, not wound or disarm, and should the assailant live or die is of no consequence providing he is no longer a lethal threat to you. The fact that an attacker didn't get his usual lucky break from an easy victim is his fault, and you can be sure that he would show you no mercy given the chance.

188

We personally think the .45 caliber semi-automatic is the best self defense handgun. If a bigger caliber was available, we would most likely recommend it over the .45. But, unfortunately, there is no handgun that has one hundred percent stopping power. A single shot from any handgun will not necessarily stop an attacker. Unless the first shot hits a vital area of the brain or spinal cord the attack could continue. A shot to the heart will sometimes instantly stop an individual, but a deranged or very excited attacker, whose body is full of adrenaline, could continue to be a lethal threat for five to fifteen seconds before he loses consciousness from falling blood pressure.

You have to keep in mind that handguns are not comparable to high powered rifles in stopping power. We seldom recommend shotguns or rifles for self defense purposes because they are awkward in close quarters, can easily be wrestled away from you, and a projectile from one of these guns can travel through several walls creating a hazard to other people. All the handguns we recommend have effective stopping power without the disadvantages of shotguns and rifles. Regardless of the type of gun or ammunition used, we recommend two consecutive shots with no hesitation in between. It is up to you to put as much on your side in respect to the caliber and the type of ammunition you choose.

You may wonder why we haven't recommended the .44 Magnum. This cartridge is the most powerful factory round available. It was designed for hunting big game animals when using a handgun. It over penetrates, causes formidable recoil, and gives off a disorientating muzzle blast and is impossible to control when rapid firing even for the strongest grip. However, if you have a .44 Magnum handgun there are some mid-range loads available such as .44 Special. This type of load makes the "44" controllable for someone who has hands large enough to handle a large revolver.

Penetration is obviously necessary but over penetration is not desirable. Over penetration would be any combination of ammunition and gun caliber in which the round would exit the body. Over penetration will not provide as much shocking power as a bullet which enters the body and remains there. The human body is easily penetrated and it is far better to use ammunition which will penetrate and possibly ricochet inside the body than one that will go straight through. More damage will be done by this type of ammunition and will provide more stopping power because the body will have to absorb the full force of the impact. You don't want ammunition which will go straight through and exit for safety reasons. If a bullet leaves an assailant's body it has to go somewhere and could possibly injure someone you were trying to protect or an innocent bystander.

The ammunition we recommend is not based on the marketing programs of its manufacturers but on police studies and our own experience and testing. There are many types of ammunition available that sound great, according to manufacturer's advertising, which simply haven't been proven or the merits have been over-inflated. We see many new types coming out all the time with claims we find hard to believe. Those which do what they claim might only work under limited conditions and, as a rule, a manufacturer will be the last to make that admission. By following our recommendation, void of any unnecessary frills, you will be using proven, reliable ammunition with maximum stopping power.

The .38 Special is used by most police departments and as a result there are a variety of different types of ammunition available for this handgun. There are ammunitions which have been designed for stopping power and their powder charge and bullet configuration provide the necessary ingredients for effective self defense.

Bullet design of handgun cartridges is a very important factor in achieving maximum stopping power. A round nose bullet will penetrate much easier than a flat nosed bullet. When choosing the proper ammunition for self defense purposes, there are other factors which must be considered before making a choice for your particular handgun. We are going to discuss the different types as well as give specific recommendations for certain guns.

The most common type of bullet is what is known as the full jacketed design. This type has the lead bullet which is cast into a specific shape and then encased in a metal jacket for the purpose of holding it together. These bullets are commonly used by the military. According to the Geneva Convention, this bullet is the most humane type of bullet. The reasoning is that the full jacketed bullet does not fragment or expand upon penetration and as a result is easier to remove from someone's body. In a self defense shooting you are not bound by the rules of the Geneva Convention and the almost comical "humane" doctrine does not apply. Your main concern is stopping the assailant and saving your life. The problem with the full jacketed bullet is that they over penetrate, endangering innocent people and does not allow you to inflict maximum stopping power on the assailant. Obviously fully jacketed bullets have limited use for self defense.

Cast bullets are made of a lead alloy and have no jacket. They are more apt to deform upon impact. Generally, during impact, they will usually deform cutting a larger wound channel and usually will not over penetrate. They have good stopping power and because of the larger wound channel will cause more severe trauma sooner than the fully jacketed bullet.

Hollow point and soft point bullets are designed to expand. They work well in smaller caliber handguns which generate high velocity with lighter bullets. The .38 Special in the "plus(+)P" load, the .357 Magnum, and .9mm generate the necessary velocity for the expansion of this

Here are some samples of different types and calibers of ammunition. Top Row: Typical 38 special and 357 magnum bullet designs. (Left to Right) semi-wadcutter, soft point and hollow point. Bottom Row: Typical 45 ACP bullet designs. (Left to Right) hardball, Hensley and Gibbs "cast" semi-wadcutter and jacketed flat nose.

bullet. These types of bullets were specifically designed for the smaller bore handguns to expand on impact. This is designed to occur when a velocity of 1,000 to 1,300 feet per second is realized. It enables the smaller caliber guns to have increased stopping power. It has been proven that the full jacketed or lead bullets do not have the stopping power that the hollow or soft point bullets do at high velocities. The only problem with this type of ammunition is that most semi-automatics will have to be modified to feed this type properly. The revolvers should not need any modification if they function properly. The only way to be certain is to test the intended ammunition at a target range and make sure it works well with your gun.

For the .38 Special and the .357 Magnum hollow point or the soft point ammunition in the "plus (+) P" or magnum loadings are highly recommended. This will give you far more stopping power than other types. However, some revolvers are not built sturdy enough to handle this powerful ammunition; you must check the manufacturer's owner's manual or with a competent gunsmith to be certain you are not creating a dangerous situation in its use. For the .45 ACP we highly recommend the lead cast Hensley and Gibbs #68 style two hundred grain semi-wadcutter. This bullet design has a flat nose with a paper cutter edge. They hit hard and do a considerable amount of damage because it cuts a large wound channel. The Hensley and Gibbs #68 is the designation of the mold used to make this type of bullet. Unfortunately there is not a major ammunition manufacturer which makes its bullets with this type of mold. As a rule, it is a mold used basically for reloads. It is possible you might find a small company in your area that uses this type, if not, a reputable manufacturer of reloads probably can be found. If you choose to load your own, it is very economical to use for both defensive ammunition and practice ammunition. For the 9mm the hollow or soft point bullets are clearly the best choice for self defense, but you will have to test their reliability in your handgun.

With the larger caliber guns such as the .45 ACP, you don't have to depend on bullet expansion for stopping power. They use a larger, heavier bullet which makes a big entry hole and wound channel. We do not recommend the hollow points which are 185-225 grains for the .45 because they will not reliably expand at the velocity of a .45 which is less than 1000 feet per second. As a result, when you compare the weight and bullet shape factors, they are a poor choice. An excellent factory load for the .45 Auto is the Hornady-Frontier ammunition loaded with a 230 Grain jacketed flat nose bullet. It is designed to feed reliably in most semi-automatics and is superior to the round nose design in stopping power.

As we have mentioned before, the .44 Magnum is not a good choice for self defense, but if you have one, when using either the acceptable .44 Special or "mid-range" loads, you should use a heavy semi-wadcutter bullet with a flat nose. These bullets make the .44 Magnum and the .44 Special very effective man stoppers.

RELOADING YOUR OWN AMMUNITION

If you do a lot of shooting, or as you practice find you will be, you should consider reloading your ammunition yourself for economic reasons. When pricing alternatives to factory ammunition you will most likely find Army surplus is almost as expensive as factory, and buying reloads from a gun shop does not offer the savings reloading yourself will.

When we say a lot of shooting we are talking about those who will be shooting at least 200 rounds a month. Any amount less than that and you might as well buy reloads. However, the savings are so great, that even those who use fewer than 200 rounds a month will eventually recoup their investment in a reloader at some point.

Basic reloading presses start out at $225.00 and include all the necessary tools and equipment. In addition to this you will need powder, primers, bullets, and brass. This will add another $75.00 to your initial investment, but keep in mind your brass can be reloaded 1 to 50 times. To illustrate to you the savings let's consider the .45 ACP ammunition. If you were to buy 1000 rounds at current factory prices, you would spend about $360.00. Once you have the brass, you can reload 1000 rounds for about $80.00. The savings will, of course, be affected by the quantity of primers, powder, and bullets you are able to purchase at one time.

Reloading is very easy to do and does not take up much room. We do not advise anyone going into business however, as in firearms products there are big liabilities, sometimes beyond the manufacturer's control, and you'll also need a federal firearms license to re-manufacture ammunition for sale. This is not to say that reloading your own is unsafe or unreliable. If you carefully reload your own ammunition, the quality will be higher than factory ammunition. We personally feel our hand loaded ammunition is more reliable and accurate. Obviously the savings are substantial, and quality can be maintained or improved.

LEATHER AND RELATED ITEMS

Holsters — When purchasing a concealment or general purpose holster, you have several things to consider. The first is the safety factor. We feel you should not purchase a holster in which the trigger guard is exposed; although, some combinations of carrying positions and guns may only allow this non-preferred type of holster. You want a holster that will firmly hold the gun in place whether you are bending or turning your body in different directions. You should not purchase a holster which clips into place on the belt. These are known as "suicide holsters" because they have a tendency to draw with the gun. You could find yourself pointing a gun still in the holster at an assailant. It's a comical picture but also deadly because you wouldn't be able to fire the weapon! The holster should be comfortable and compatible with the type of clothing you wear to maintain not only your personal comfort but concealment also. You will be limited in the types of clothing you can wear with certain types of carrying positions.

TED BLOCKER CUSTOM HOLSTERS

Body Guard — It will fit semi-automatics or revolvers and is teflon lined. This feature allows for a smooth draw and does not sweat like leather holsters which can cause the gun to rust. This holster incorporates a thumb snap release and must be unsnapped before the weapon can be drawn.

Security — This is another example of Ted Blocker's exacting demand for quality. This holster is also teflon lined and can be used with semi-automatics and revolvers. It is an open top holster that depends on friction fit. The friction fit is accomplished by an adjustable tension device engineered into its design to firmly hold the weapon in place.

X-16 — This is one of the best all around holsters made and can be purchased for the semi-automatic or the revolver. It is an external belt holster of very high quality that can be worn on the strong side or the crossdraw position. It has an adjustable tension providing maximum stability.

Dalton #10 Hideout — This is an inside the pants holster designed by co-author Mike Dalton. It is constructed to keep the rear sight from snagging on clothing or gouging the body while being worn. It has a swivel belt attachment which will allow the wearer to adjust the position while being worn. It is very comfortable, and we feel it is the best inside the pants holster on the market and can be used with the semi-automatic or the revolver with a two to four inch barrel.

RENEGADE LEATHER

Cozy Partner — If you wish to utilize the ankle carry, this holster is an excellent choice. Model #50 for two inch revolvers is an absolute jewel. It is made with nylon elastic with full velcro fastening bands. It has good weapon retention yet allows for a fast and smooth draw. Also, it tucks the "butt" close into the calf without a jabbing effect and is very comfortable. This holster, unlike many others, uses the trigger guard to retain the handgun. This is an important consideration because a two inch .38 for concealed carry will most likely have the hammer spur removed making it impossible to utilize a hammer safety strap.

MAGAZINES

Only purchase magazines that are made by your firearm's manufacturer. We don't recommend your purchasing any of the extended magazines you may come across. Most are not reliable enough for a life-saving situation. Take your pistol with you to try out any magazines to see that they fall out of the pistol from their own weight. (This is mainly applicable to the Colt .45 semi-automatic but pistols without magazine disconnectors or bottom release catches will allow them to fall out freely.)

The "Dalton Hideout" is available in smooth finish or "rough out" for re- *volvers or auto-pistols. Also, pictured is one of Ted's high quality belts.*

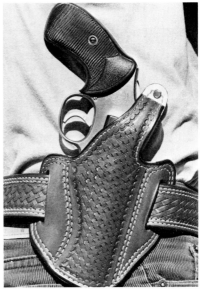

The "X-16" general purpose holster.

The "Body Guard kidney position holster.

MAGAZINE POUCHES

For concealed carry, a single magazine pouch is quite useful, and can be concealed with relative ease. Here we recommend Ted Blocker's "Tef-loc" magazine pouch. It has a spring steel retainer that is teflon coated to provide excellent retention while allowing a smooth, quick draw. It is also low cut to allow a proper grip on the magazine and to ensure that you do not fumble or drop a much needed magazine.

SPEEDLOADERS

HKS Speedloader — You would most likely want this item for home use or at your place of business. It is not generally suitable for concealed carry because of the bulk.

Bianchi Model 580 "Speed Strip" — This is very concealable and allows for the loading of one or two cartridges at a time without the danger of dropping them. It fits easily in any pocket.

The Bianchi "Speed Strip" is well designed.

Cartridges are loaded two at a time.

BELTS

A sturdy belt is a very important factor in being able to carry a weapon concealed on your person. When you buy a belt for this purpose, don't try to over economize. A proper belt will run between ten and thirty dollars and over the long run will turn out to be less expensive than a cheaper belt which will not hold up very long by comparison. Ted Blocker's belts are highly recommended.

We have specifically recommended Ted Blocker equipment because we have been directly involved in the designing process of that equipment, and naturally feel it is top quality, meeting and exceeding all necessary requirements. However, equipment manufactured by Gordon Davis or Milt Sparks are of high quality and custom made. Bianchi Leather or Rogers Holster Company markets production leather and generally is less expensive than custom equipment, but maintain high quality and are all good choices for your leather needs. You might want to write for all the brochures and then make your decision following our guidelines.

ANSWERS TO "GOOD TACTICS" SCENE:

1. She has kept good distance from the attacker and kept his head where he can't see her.

2. She is partially concealed and her back is toward an area she has previously cleared.

3. She has commanded the attacker to keep his hands on his head with fingers interlocked and nose to the floor.

4. Strong hand keeps him covered while she contacts the police and could drop the phone and use both hands to fire if necessary.

5. She, also, keeps her eyes on the attacker at all times.

6. Although she can see his obvious weapon, she must assume that he may be carrying other weapons or could even use the wine bottle against her.

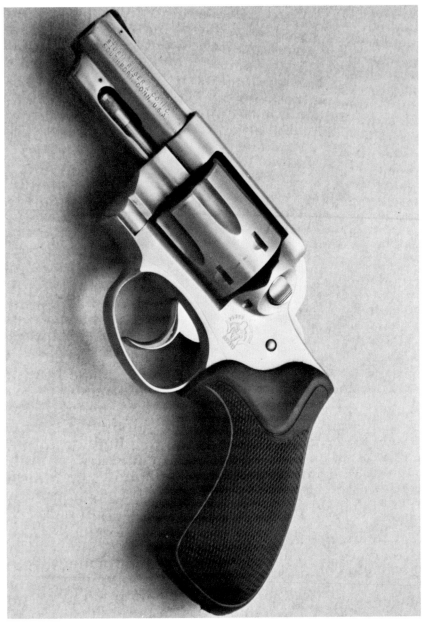

An example of a "fully tuned" and modified Ruger revolver customized by Ron Power. A gun like this is a real pleasure to shoot.

CHAPTER 9

MODIFICATIONS

Modifications will literally customize your handgun to suit your individual needs. Modifications can only be done on a handgun that is already in good working condition. If you buy a used gun, have a gunsmith check it to make sure the weapon is mechanically sound before having any modifications done. The modifications we will discuss should cost (as of date of publication) in the range of fifty to seventy dollars. Some of these modifications will help you fire the weapon in a more accurate manner and as a result help build your confidence in the weapon and your ability to use it effectively.

REVOLVERS

Revolvers are made at the factory with the grip which fits the "average" individual. Few of us seem to fit the manufacturers concept of average. When you buy a revolver, you will most likely find that the grip will either be too large or too small. For accurate shooting, it is very important that the gun feels right in your hand. There are many grip handles available through a number of manufacturers. We have found that some of the best revolver grips are made by Pachmayr. These grips are made from a rubber material and come in different shapes and sizes and are adaptable to all the guns we recommend. They allow you to get a good, snug, slip free grip on the handle as well as greatly aid in the absorption of recoil. This is particularly important in some of the lighter revolvers where the recoil is most noticeable. Also Hogue Combat Grips Inc., makes find quality grips for the revolver and semi-automatics. They are available in a number of different materials, and are both durable and attractive.

There are several guidelines to follow when selecting a grip. First, when you grip the gun high up on the back strap, centered properly in the web of your hand, your trigger finger should naturally fall into the

199

proper position. You should be able to fully wrap your hand around the grip. The more of your hand you can get on the grip itself, the more control you will have to make quick recovery shots.

There are other manufacturers who make wooden grips with different sizes and shapes. Everyone has a preference and the only way for you to make the right decision is to go to a gun shop and try the available alternatives. The most important thing is that the revolver feels right in your hand.

Another consideration which will effect your choice is the type of gun you own. As we have mentioned before, there are two basic designs; one is the round butt and the other is the square butt. The round butt is easier to handle if you have small hands and can be more easily concealed than the square butt. The square butt fits larger hands and can take larger grip panels. The square butt design is suitable for a home protection gun, providing your hands are large enough. We do, however, recommend the rubber grip for any gun over the wooden grip, because they afford you more control over recoil no matter what butt design you may have.

The trigger pull on the revolver is a modification which is very important and yet inexpensive. The double action revolver trigger pull is very long and heavy compared to the semi-automatic pistol. The trigger pull weight is in the area of eight to fourteen pounds whereas the semi-automatic is only approximately half this weight or less. A novice won't be able to pick up a gun for the first time and know whether or not it needs a trigger job. As you practice dry firing and working with the gun, you will get a better feel for the way it works. If, while dry firing using a coin balanced on the front sight, you feel you are having problems pulling the trigger smoothly, you should probably have it reworked. A smooth pull on the trigger is very important for accurate shooting. Some revolvers come from the factory with a smooth trigger pull, but again, they are designed for the "average" shooter. More than likely you will get one in need of modification. Take it to a gunsmith and tell him you want the double action smoothed out for defensive use. You don't want the gunsmith to modify the trigger pull for competition use only. Trigger modifications for competition are made as light as possible and because of this the hammer sometimes does not strike the primer of the cartridge hard enough for ignition. This causes misfires and obviously reliability is most important for defensive shooting. In general, the pull weight on the trigger should not be below eight pounds on the defensive revolver.

The trigger itself is another area where a simple modification can increase your accuracy. Most triggers come from the factory, whether narrow or wide, with serrations or horizontal grooves on the trigger. These serrations tend to impede a smooth, steady pull on the trigger. They also tend to chew up softer skinned fingers. Unless you don't mind wearing a bandage on your trigger finger, it is a very simple process for a gunsmith to smooth and polish the trigger.

When selecting your revolver, try to choose a model which doesn't have the wide target style trigger. If the model you choose has a wide trigger, have it replaced with a narrow style trigger. On most revolvers, these parts are interchangeable. The narrow trigger is easier to use and more precisely manipulated in double action shooting.

If you do have your trigger modified, it is absolutely necessary to test fire the gun. Go to a target range and shoot approximately two hundred rounds of reliable ammunition. If you have any problems, take it back to the gunsmith and then repeat the test to make sure the problem was corrected.

A word of caution. Don't let your gunsmith talk you into putting a trigger stop on your revolver. A trigger stop is an adjustable screw which limits the amount of overtravel on the trigger after firing. If that little screw should ever work itself loose, the gun might not fire.

Most defensive shooting situations are ten feet or less and your revolver will only be used in the double action mode. Generally the only time the defensive revolver is used single action is to deliver precise mid to long range fire. For defensive shooting, the single action mode takes too much time between shots to be effective. This is why we recommend that you have your revolver set up to be the most effective when firing double action.

Even with a trigger job and the pressure set at eight pounds, some people will find it difficult, at first, to pull the trigger smoothly. Don't get discouraged. As you practice, the necessary muscles in your fingers, hand and forearm will develop. In a short period of time, you will be able to smoothly pull the trigger with a minimal disturbance of the sight picture and the accuracy of your shooting will improve.

Another valuable modification is known as dehorning the hammer. This involves cutting off the thumb cocking spur and smoothing off the back of the hammer. The reasons for doing this are mainly to eliminate any interference when you grip high on the revolver between the web of your hand and the hammer. This is an absolute necessity if you are going to carry the gun concealed, as a hammer which isn't dehorned can catch on clothing or the sides of a purse. Some of the smaller revolvers such as the .38 Special, have what is known as a shrouded hammer and are designed for maximum concealability. A shrouded hammer is enclosed by the frame around the hammer and doesn't need modification.

Some people find that a simple modification to the front sight, such as the installation of a color insert, makes it easier to quickly focus on the sight. Your local gunsmith probably has a good selection of colors. The most popular colors are orange, yellow and a fluorescent red. If you don't wish to spend the money, any similar brightly colored fingernail polish will also work. We personally recommend fluorescent orange model airplane paint that can be purchased at a hobby shop. A color insert is especially helpful when shooting in low light. If you are having trouble picking up your front sight, this is something to consider.

SEMI-AUTOMATICS

The semi-automatic pistol is, for the most part, a more complicated handgun with options and standard features varying depending on the model and the manufacturer. We, therefore, can not generalize on modifications as with the double action revolvers. For this reason we will discuss only the Colt Mark IV Government model .45. We chose this particular make and model because it has proven its reliability and durability under the extreme demands of combat shooting and is also a model that allows us to discuss all possible modifications in relation to defensive shooting. Other models are in our chapter on recommended guns.

We can make one generalization, however, in reference to the type of finish on the weapon you purchase. Do not buy a semi-automatic with a nickel finish. Many gunsmiths will refuse to work on a gun with a nickel finish. Always get the blue finish. The reason is the nickel finish will have to be stripped away before modifications can be made. If a gunsmith does agree to work on it, you will find you have an unnecessary expense of having to replate it after the work is done.

The factory grips on the semi-automatic Colt do have a good feel. Still the size might not be right for you. If you don't shoot a lot or are bothered by the recoil, you might prefer the Pachmayr rubber grips. These grips will help to absorb some of the recoil. If you have large hands, you might want to try the "Breskovich" grip panels which are designed for larger hands. As a rule, the recoil on most .45 semi-automatics will not be intense enough to go the expense of the rubber grips, but this is something only you can decide.

On the back of the grip on a semi-automatic is what is known as the mainspring housing. The regular Mark IV, from the factory, has an arched mainspring housing. This fills up the palm of your hand and works fine for people with medium to large hands. If your hands are not large enough to fully enclose this housing, there is a part known as a flat mainspring housing which is a "drop in part" and doesn't require any extra fitting. This will enable those with small hands to encompass the grip and control the recoil better. Try the weapon out, see how it feels in your hand. If you can comfortably get your index finger in the proper position on the trigger, you probably don't need this modification. If you can't, or it feels awkward, you will have to make the suggested grip modifications.

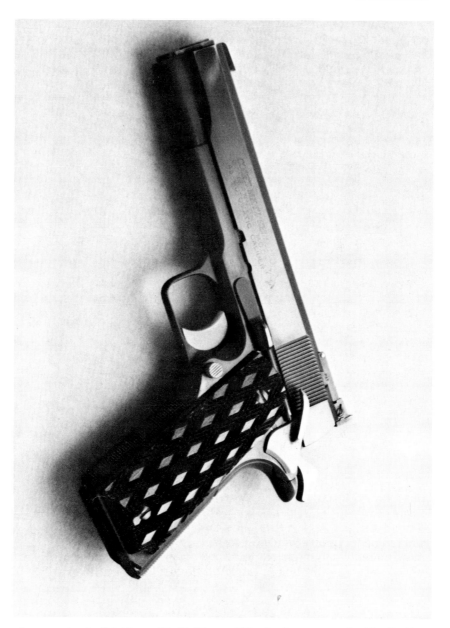

An example of a "highly modified" .45 auto. This pistol was customized by Jim Hoag and can bring you many hours of enjoyment at the target range as well as be a good self defense weapon.

Once the pistol fits well in your hand, the next consideration is the position of the safety. This particular model comes with a small safety and is only comfortably operated by right handed people. There are ambidextrous safetys available which can be used by anyone. The best available ambidextrous safety is made by Armand Swenson. There is also a "speed safety" available for this model. This type of safety is similar to the standard safety except the lever is larger and this makes it easier to quickly take the safety "off." We only recommend this type of safety if you have problems disengaging the standard one. We recommend against this safety if you intend to carry your gun concealed. You could find that the safety has been accidentally pushed "off" and you have been walking around without the safety "on."

If you wish to carry your pistol concealed, we recommend a Colt Ambidextrous Safety which is readily available. It is a standard size safety that can be operated by left or right handed persons. When carrying a gun, you should always make sure that your safety isn't so loose that it takes almost no effort to flip it "on" or "off." This is of extreme importance for obvious safety reasons.

When you first purchase a new weapon, you should always take it to a range and fire it with different types of ammunition. This is an important step to assure the reliability of your weapon. Try a round nose type of ammunition first and if it works well with this type, then try it with semi wadcutter ammunition and hollow point ammunition. If your weapon is reliable with all these different ammunition types, then you are one of the few lucky people who have bought the one in a thousand pistol which works perfectly right out of the box from the manufacturer. Most likely you will find that your gun will not work well with certain bullet shapes. This will require some work on the ramping and throating. "Ramping" is the feed ramp inside the frame of the gun that the nose of the bullet slides along out of the magazine. This may need to be polished and cut at the proper angle. A gunsmith can do this for you and this will assure that the nose of the bullet feeds up into the throat of the barrel reliably. "Throating" refers to the throat of the barrel. This sometimes requires a little of the metal on the bottom of the barrel relieved to allow different bullet shapes to move smoothly and reliably into the chamber. These modifications must only be done by an experienced gunsmith. You can ruin the barrel or the frame by attempting to do this yourself or by allowing someone not familiar with a .45 semi-automatic to do it. Always test with at least three magazines to be certain that the weapon is the problem, not the magazines.

Another modification is lowering the ejection port. The ejection port is the cut out portion of the slide where the empty casing is ejected when the gun is fired. When the ejection port is too high, it can cause the case to stick rather than eject not only resulting in damage to the casing but also jamming the gun. Another advantage of this modification is that it will cause your empty cases to eject more to the side than to the rear. It can be dangerous and painful to have brass flying back into your face with every shot you fire. You also want to make sure that the tension on the extractor is adjusted so that it holds the rim of the case properly to give you positive ejection.

Another important modification is a crisp trigger pull. We have discussed the importance of a trigger pull which is as smooth as possible and by crisp we mean a trigger pull where there is no sluggishness or hesitation as the trigger is pulled. You should feel tension in the trigger and a smoothness so as you pull you feel the tension much as you would with a light switch. The weight of pull in the semi-automatic trigger should be in the three and one half to four pound range, free of any sluggishness in the pull. The length of the trigger might also have to be tailored to your hand size and be done at the same time you have any trigger work done. The Colt Mark IV comes from the factory with a short trigger. The short trigger usually works very well for those with small hands. People with a medium to large hand will probably find they like the feel of a longer trigger better.

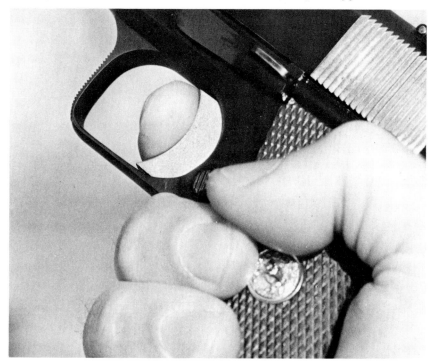

The match length trigger is an aid to better marksmanship for those with average to large hands.

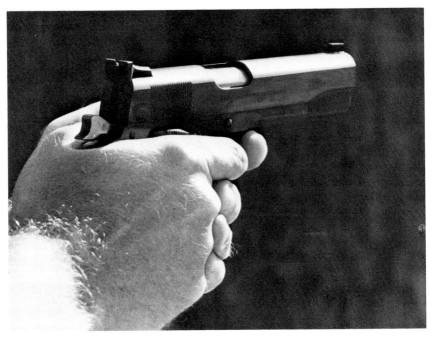

One of the finest "fixed sights" available for the .45 auto is made by Armand Swenson. This sight system gives an excellent sight picture and is quick to "pick up" for follow up shots.

Before you have trigger work done, get a feel for the trigger. If it has a good feel, leave it alone. Have your trigger set around four pounds. The Colt Mark IV does not come from the factory with a trigger stop. The long aluminum match triggers do come with a trigger stop and if your gun has one be sure to have it "lock-tited" or crimped to insure that the set screw doesn't work itself loose and be sure to check it regularly. If you don't want to be bothered with checking it occasionally, then have it removed entirely.

The sights are another area which needs modification. The Colt has very small front and rear sights which are difficult to pick up quickly and almost impossible to pick up in low light. You should have a set of high visibility fixed sights installed. We recommend the Swenson fixed sight. The sight slot on the rear is known as a dovetail and the Swenson sight can be installed without any machining. On the front of the slide, you should have what is known as an improved ramp front sight installed with .125 inches width. You need to have a competent gunsmith do this. That front sight should not be "staked" in. It must be silver soldered or welded into a machined channel or it is likely to fly off during recoil.

A desirable modification but one not absolutely necessary is to bevel the magazine well. This will allow for quicker and smoother reloading of fresh magazines. What this will do is chamfer the magazine well opening. If cost is a factor in your modification, this is the last thing you would want to have done. If you can afford it, it can prove very helpful.

As you learn more about semi-automatics, you will have people tell you a variety of different things about the recoil springs. They will, more often than not, tell you to have a heavier recoil spring installed. We do not agree with this theory. Standard Colt springs function just fine and there is no need to go to the additional expense of purchasing a heavier recoil spring.

If you have large hands, a modification known as "bobbing the hammer" is something to seriously consider. The web of larger hands sometimes rides up over the grip and this can be both dangerous and painful. If the web of your hand gets caught during the rechambering action of the slide, it can be cut quite deeply. By bobbing the hammer, you will have the hammer cut back so it won't come into contact with the web of your hand. It can be very distracting to know you are shooting a gun which can cause pain and discomfort. This can cause flinching and a variety of other undesirable habits which will seriously affect your ability to shoot accurately. This very inexpensive modification can take care of the problem easily.

All of the modifications we have discussed for the semi-automatic pistol should cost no more than a maximum of two hundred dollars. As you can see, the semi-automatic is considerably more expensive to modify than the revolver. All modifications should only be done by a reputable, competent gunsmith. We can't stress enough that gunsmithing is not something for "do it yourselfers." You can ruin a gun, just as easily as an incompetent gunsmith, not to mention create a dangerous situation.

There are other modifications you can do to both the revolver and the semi-automatic. No matter how competent a gunsmith is, he is in the business of selling his products and work and will likely try to sell you everything under the sun. On the .45 semi-automatic, for instance, you can spend anywhere from zero to fifteen hundred on modifications. But, fortunately, for a top notch defensive handgun, you only need to do the modifications we have discussed.

CARE AND MAINTENANCE

Your self defense handgun is a high precision mechanism. Its accuracy and reliability are dependent on its proper care and maintenance. It represents both a financial investment and an investment in your ability to defend your life. We strongly advise you to follow the guidelines in this chapter, as well as any and all manufacturer suggestions for the care and maintenance of your particular model and make. If you buy a used gun, you should be able to purchase a maintenance guide through a gun shop. You can also order this guide by writing the manufacturer.

Revolvers are vulnerable to abuse due to the fact that many of their moving parts are exposed. As sturdy and sound as they seem to be, it doesn't take much in the way of carelessness to negatively affect their performance. For example, a broken or bent hammer spur may not allow the gun to fire. A bent trigger will make it difficult, if not impossible, to properly pull the trigger. Bent sights will drastically reduce their usefulness. A bent ejector rod could prevent the cylinder from rotating or make it impossible to unload spent rounds. Revolvers also have more moving parts than semi-automatics, these being the many levers involved in the rotation of the cylinder, which can jam if foreign particles get in the gun.

As a rule, these problems are caused by carelessness and unfortunate accidents such as dropping the revolver. They can also be caused by rough handling. When loading and unloading, don't snap open the cylinder or slam it shut. This will induce problems. The synchronization of the cylinder could be affected, thereby failing to lock itself in the proper position. The cartridges will not be aligned properly which will affect accuracy as well as create a safety hazard. The crane or yoke could also be damaged by slamming the cylinder. You can avoid this by smoothly and slowly opening and closing the cylinder.

Periodically you should check the following on your revolver:

1. Check the clearance between the trigger and trigger guard. Do this by double action dry firing. It should work smoothly and freely.
2. Open the cylinder and check for freedom of movement. There should be no hitches in the back and forth movement and it should spin freely.
3. The ejector rod should be inspected for straightness. A slight bend might not be visible so work it back and forth checking to see that it operates without binding throughout its entire movement.
4. Check all screws on the gun to be certain they have not worked loose. There is a great deal of force absorbed by the entire gun when fired and from time to time they will have to be tightened.
5. Any time the muzzle of your gun touches the ground or a surface with debris make sure the barrel is clear before firing the weapon.
6. Do all of this whenever you drop or mishandle your weapon.

The semi-automatics, although durable, still can develop potential problems if the gun is abused or dropped. Slamming the magazine could bend the lips of the magazine, making it unable to properly feed the rounds. The same can happen if the magazine is dropped or stored or carried in such a way that it bounces around against other objects.

Therefore, when loading don't slam the magazine, this includes reloading under fire. Practice sliding the magazine into place with a firm but steady motion. This will not adversely effect your speed. Carry your magazines secured in such a way that they won't bounce around in your equipment bag. Magazines not in use should be kept empty or with one round in them to protect the follower. If a magazine is bent, pitted, or has a loose floor plate, throw it away. You don't want to possibly mix it with reliable magazines. If it is a marginal defect, perhaps only superficial, which does not seem to affect performance, it would be best to only use it for practice purposes. Next to ammunition, magazines are the most common problem with the semi-automatics.

If you should drop the pistol, you could break or misalign the sights. Also, some semi-automatics can not be dry fired. Check the manufacturer's guidelines. You might have to insert an empty cartridge to avoid breaking the firing pin. Do not let the slide slam down from the slide lock, when the pistol is empty; this will ruin the hammer and sear engagement. Tripping the slide stop and letting it fall of its own weight is only advisable when chambering a fresh round from a magazine.

Periodically you should check the following on the auto-pistol:

1. Check magazines for the problems we described.
2. Check for small cracks in parts of the weapon.
3. Check the sights.
4. Check for smooth slide action.
5. If it is not properly chambering the rounds and you are sure the ammunition and magazine isn't the problem, have the gun checked by a gunsmith.
6. Recheck steps one through four if you drop or mishandle the weapon.

MALFUNCTIONS

If you have a malfunction at the range, your target will wait while you check out the problem. If you have a malfunction during a confrontation, you have to think fast. If you have properly cared for your handgun and are using ammunition which is in dependable condition, you should not be faced with this problem. But even when all the proper steps are taken "Murphy's Law" can still pop up.

If the handgun fails to fire, the first thing you should do is take your finger completely off the trigger and let it return completely to the full forward position. If you are firing rapid shots it is possible, when taking into consideration the stress involved, you simply have not released the trigger sufficiently. This will make the trigger seem as if it is jammed. With a full release, you will eliminate this problem or at least you will be able to go to the next checkpoint.

The next step would be to eject all ammunition and reload. You could have bad ammunition or a high primer or you may unknowingly be trying to fire a gun which is empty. Unless you have the misfortune of your handgun breaking down at the worst possible time, these steps should solve the problem.

The semi-automatic is more sensitive to the ammunition it is fed than the revolver, and therefore most feeding problems are a direct result of the ammunition. If you properly care for your weapon, the magazines, and carefully select your ammunition, you can effectively eliminate this problem. Once in a while a weak charge, bad primer, or improperly loaded ammunition will cause some type of malfunction.

CLEANING YOUR WEAPON

Cleaning your handgun is a chore. We can't even make it sound like fun, and we doubt even Tom Sawyer could. But, it is critical if you want your handgun to remain dependable. A gun which is dirty and poorly cared for can quickly become a liability rather than a life saving asset. If you take care of your gun, you can also avoid the need for expensive repair work. The functional aspects of any gun can be maintained for decades with proper care and cleaning.

All guns are exposed to elements which can cause mechanical malfunctions. Unless a gun is stored in a total vacuum, the combination of air, moisture and dust mandate cleaning on a regular basis. When you shoot, every shot leaves behind a residue of powder and lead particles. Add to these factors sweat and body oils and you can clearly see why you must clean your gun on a regular basis. From a financial standpoint it is much cheaper to purchase the cleaning materials you will need than to put this off until the gun needs the inevitable repairs which stem from neglecting to take care of the weapon.

When you clean your handgun make sure you do it in a clean, lint free environment. A kitchen or utility room or a workshop area in your garage will serve this purpose. Privacy should be a consideration when deciding where you are going to clean your handgun. If you have taken your gun apart, the last thing you want is someone interrupting you or a small child walking off with one of the components.

Any gun shop will have cleaning kits on hand. Make sure the kit you buy is a complete kit specifically designed to clean the type of gun and caliber you own. If you aren't sure and the store won't guarantee that it is, then look for another kit. Makeshift equipment can do more harm than good. Many people try to save a few pennies on the cost of the cleaning kit and end up wishing they hadn't. They have ended up using the wrong solvent or bore brush and succeeded in only damaging their gun. A rule of thumb to follow is never use a cleaning tool which is harder than the surface to be cleaned and don't pinch pennies or you will end up squandering dollars.

Basically your equipment will include:

1. Screwdrivers which will fit the screws on your gun.
2. Clean rags or towels.
3. A scraping tool, such as a dentist probe. (Ask your dentist for an old one.)
4. A small nylon brush, such as a toothbrush.
5. Gun cleaning solvent, but high grade quality solvent. (Ask the gunsmith which solvent is best for your gun.)
6. Gun oil, a high grade oil specifically designed for guns.
7. A silicone treated cloth, these cloths are lint free.
8. A bore brush of the correct caliber.
9. A cleaning rod.
10. Cleaning patches.
11. "Q-tips."

Before you start to clean your gun think about safety. **Assume it is loaded!** Never take the chance and proceed without checking to make sure that it is unloaded. We strongly suggest that you put any ammunition a reasonable distance from the weapon. Keep the muzzle pointed away from yourself and anything else you don't want destroyed. If you must leave the gun unattended, put the weapon and all the parts in an area away from other people in the house. Always observe all the safety procedures we've discussed in the safety chapter. Even after you take your gun apart and put it back together, check it again to make sure it's not loaded before you dry fire it.

When you actually begin the cleaning process, keep in mind you are working with very strong solvents and high grade oils which can stain clothing, fabrics, wood surfaces, as well as being rather offensive to the human nose. Old clothing and a ventilated area are a very good idea. If you are working on a table or counter you don't want stained, then place plastic on it and lay absorbent towels on top of the plastic. This way the work surface won't be stained and the towels will soak up anything that might run onto the floor below.

The actual cleaning process and how often it should be done will vary according to manufacturer guidelines. For that reason we feel it is better for you to follow those specific guidelines rather than any generalized information we provide. If you have bought a used gun and don't have the manufacturer's guidelines, check with your local gun shop or write directly to the manufacturer for one.

Some tips which apply to all guns are when you disassemble your gun clean all the parts in a cleaning solvent and dry them out thoroughly. "Q-tips" are great for those very hard to get to nooks and crannies. It is important when oiling your gun not to leave any excess. Oil will contaminate the ammunition creating obvious problems. Magazines need only a very light oiling, and all excess must be cleaned off. In extremely cold weather, oil can become a heavy grease which can cause the moving parts to work sluggishly at best. If you are storing your gun in a cold place, you are better off using a small amount of dry graphite. By cold, we're talking in terms of temperatures below zero. Dry graphite should not be used other than these conditions as it does not provide sufficient lubrication. We strongly advise against dismantling your gun beyond the steps suggested by the manufacturer. Both the revolver and the semi-automatic reach a point at which it is no longer a simple process, and you might very well find yourself with a useless gun you can't put back together without the expense of enlisting the aid of a gunsmith.

After you have cleaned your gun out and put it back together, check your work visually, and then dry fire the gun to make sure all the components are working smoothly. As a rule, you should clean your gun after practicing. Once you have cleaned your gun a few times, you will find the task quite simple and relatively easy.

CONCLUSION

You should now have an understanding of the shooting techniques and the tactics involved for use of the handgun for self-defense. Some things will be more clear as you practice to develop skills and begin your tactical pre-planning.

If at any time you find yourself not shooting as well as you know you can, go back to the fundamentals. This will usually correct whatever problem seems to have arisen. If not, check thoroughly all your equipment for proper working order. There are no "great mysteries" to solve these problems; logic and determination will succeed.

We would like to say once more that you must exercise "common sense" in the use of lethal force. Also, remember to always handle your firearms with extreme regard to your safety and to the safety of others.

It is indeed our sincere hope that the information contained in this book will save many lives and provide many with a more secure way of life.

RESOURCE GUIDE

Manufacturers-Suppliers

Advanced .45 Technology Inc.
(Firing Simulator)
1031 Elder Street
Oxnard, CA 93030
(805) 485-0113

Advantage Accessories
(Grip Panels)
Jack Breskovich
P.O. Box 828
Whittier, CA 90608
(213) 695-4134

Auto-Ordnance
West Hurley (Pistols)
New York 12491
(914) 679-7225

Bar-Sto Precision
(Stainless Steel Barrels)
73377 Sullivan Rd.
Twentynine Palms, CA 92277
(619) 367-2747

Bianchi Gunleather
100 Calle Cortez
Temecula, CA 92390
(714) 676-5621

Ted Blocker's Custom Holsters
4939 Santa Anita Ave.
Temple City, CA 91780
(818) 442-5772

Cannon Safe Company
9358 Stephens
Pico Rivera, CA 90660
1-800-242-4028

Charter Arms Corp. (Revolvers)
430 Sniffens Lane
Stratford, Conn. 06497

Colt Firearms
(Pistols and Revolvers)
Talcott Rd.
West Hartford, Conn. 06110

G. Wm. Davis
(Custom Leather)
3930 Valley Blvd. (F)
Walnut, CA 91789
(714) 598-5620

Detonics (Pistols)
2500 Seattle Tower
Seattle, WA 98101
(206) 747-2100

HKS Products
(Speedloaders) 132 Fifth St.
Dayton, KY 41074

Hogue Combat Grips Inc.
P.O. Box 2035
Atascadero, CA 93422

Hornady Manufacturing Co.
P.O. Box 1848
Grand Island, NE 68802

International Shootists Inc.
P.O. Box 5254
Mission Hills, CA 91345
(818) 891-1723

Pachmayr Gun Works
(Rubberized Grips)
1220 S. Grand Ave.
Los Angeles, CA 90015

Randall Firearms
P.O. Box 728
Sun Valley, CA 91352

Renegade Holster Co.
(Ankle Holster)
P.O. Box 31546
Phoenix, AZ 85046
(602) 971-5900

Rogers Holster Co.
1736 St. Johns Bluff Rd.
Jacksonville, FL 32216
1-800-874-1610

Smith & Wesson
2100 Roosevelt Ave.
Springfield, Mass. 01101

Milt Sparks
(Custom Leather)
Box 187
Idaho City, ID 83631

Sturm Ruger and Co. Inc.
(Revolvers)
Southport, Conn. 06490
(203) 259-7843

T.M. Industries
(Silhouette Targets)
P.O. Box 68
Santa Monica, CA 90406
(213) 454-9440

**Semi-Automatic Gunsmiths
and Custom Parts:**

B & B Sales
Luis Urrutia
12521 Oxnard St.
No. Hollywood, CA 91606
(818) 985-2329

Jim Boland
15735 Strathern
Unit 5
Van Nuys, CA 91406
(818) 893-8972

Ed Brown
Route 1, Box 153
Perry, MO 63462
(314) 565-3261

Jim Clark
Rte. 2, Box 22-A
Keithville, LA 71047
(318) 925-0836

Competition Systems
1001 Building E Hensley St.
Richmond, CA 94809
(415) 237-3110

Bob Greider
4625 Carrie Ann Lane
Abilene, TX 79606
(915) 698-2006

Richard Heinie—Pistolsmith
821 E. Adams
Havana, IL 62644

James W. Hoag
8523 Canoga Ave.
Canoga Park, CA 91304
(818) 998-1510

Don Nygord
6278 Hamilton Lane
La Crescenta, CA 91214
(818) 352-3027

J. Michael Plaxco
Roland Cut-Off
Roland, AR
(501) 868-9767

John Spilborghs
1110 E. De la Guerra
Santa Barbara, CA 93103-1529
(805) 965-0701 after 4:00 p.m.

Armand Swenson
P.O. Box 606
Fallbrook, CA 92028
(714) 728-5319

Mike Tibbet
4737 Ortega
Ventura, CA 93006
(805) 985-0628

Wilson's
Route 3, Box 211D
Berryville, AR 72616
(501) 545-3618

**Revolver Gunsmiths
and Custom Parts:**

B & B Sales
Luis Urrutia
12521 Oxnard St.
No. Hollywood, CA 91606
(818) 985-2329

Cannon's Guns
Andy Cannon
P.O. Box 357, Rte. 93
Victor, MT 59875
(406) 642-3861

Davis Custom Guns
Bill & Gil Davis
2793 Delmonte St.
West Sacramento, CA 95691
(916) 372-6789

Jim Clark
Rte. 2, Box 22-A
Keithville, LA 71047
(318) 925-0836

Joe K's
Joe Kassay & Jim Arbes
500 High St.
Perthamboy, NJ 08861
(201) 442-4414

Mag-na-port Arms
Larry Kelly
30016 S. River Rd.
Mt. Clemens, MI 48045
(313) 469-6727

Maryland Gunworks Ltd.
P.O. Box 130
Clarksburg, MD 20871

Power Custom Inc.
Ron Power
Box 1604
Independence, MO 64055
(816) 833-3102

Robert A. McGrew
3315 Michigan Ave.
Colorado Springs, CO 80910

Wilson's
Rte 3, Box 211D
Berryville, AR 72616
(501) 545-3618

GLOSSARY OF TERMS

Action: Mechanism used to load and unload and fire the weapon.

Ballistics: The firing characteristics of firearms, bullets, and cartridges.

Barrel: Cylindrical tube through which a projectile travels.

Base Pad: An object usually made of leather or rubber placed on the bottom of a magazine to ensure proper seating.

Bore: The inside diameter of the barrel.

Bullet: A shaped piece of metal that is fitted in a cartridge and shot from a firearm.

Bull Barrel: Heavy barrel, larger than normal.

Butt: The blunt, thick handle-like part of the handgun grasped by the hand, consisting of the frame and stocks.

Caliber: The inside diameter of the bore of a barrel.

Canted: Holding the handgun at an angle.

Cartridge: Cylindrical case of metal containing the powder and projectile for a firearm.

Chamber: The part of the gun that holds the cartridge(s).

Checkered: A uniform rough pattern embossed into steel or wood to provide a better grip.

Cock: To raise the hammer of the gun into firing position.

Cover: An object that would provide concealment that is bullet-proof.

Cylinder: The rotating part of a revolver where the cartridges are contained.

Concealment: An object that would hide you but would not be bullet-proof.

Double-Action Revolver: A type of revolver that can be fired by trigger cocking or thumb cocking.

Double-Action Semi-Automatic: A pistol designed to be carried hammer down with a round in the chamber. The first shot is fired by trigger cocking the hammer; the remaining cartridges are fired single action.

Ejector: A device within the action that removes the empty casing(s) from the chamber(s).

Ejection Port: The opening on the slide where the spent casing is expelled.

Extractor: A device that removes an empty case from the chamber.

Firearm: A hand held weapon which is discharged by an explosive.

Firing Pin: A pin that strikes the cartridge primer in the chamber of a firearm when it is fired.

Follower: The platform inside the magazine that guides the ammunition upwards.

Grip: The manner in which you place your hand on the gun to steady the weapon.

Grip Safety: A device designed to prevent the handgun from being fired unless it is properly held by the operator.

Hammer: A part of the action, driven by the mainspring, that when actuated by the trigger causes the firing pin to strike the primer, igniting the powder charge.

Hollow Point: A type of expanding bullet.

Kick: Recoil.

Load: The exact specifications for a cartridge such as weight and caliber size. To "load" a weapon is to place a cartridge into the firing chamber.

Magazine: A device for semi-automatic pistols that holds additional cartridges ready for use.

Magnum: A cartridge design intended to develop a higher velocity than cartridges of the same bore diameter.

Mainspring: The spring which drives the firing mechanism of a firearm.

Muzzle: Barrel opening of a firearm.

Off-Hand: A standing position with no artificial support whatsoever.

Piece: Slang expression for any firearm.

Pistol: A handgun. Commonly used to describe a semi-automatic handgun.

Power: In handguns, the force expended by a cartridge when fired in a specific weapon.

Primer: Ignition cap on the rear end of a cartridge.

Range: The distance a bullet will travel before losing its initial momentum. Also, a place for shooting at targets.

Recoil: "To every action there must be an equal and opposite reaction." — Newton. A backward motion of the weapon resulting from the firing of a round. Also known as kick.

Recoil Spring: The spring, or springs, that returns the action into battery after the discharge of a semi-automatic weapon.

Revolver: A pistol having chambers in a rotating cylinder for holding several cartridges that may be fired in succession.

Rim: A collar around the cartridge head which gives the extractor a hook-hold.

Round: One cartridge, one shot.

Round Nose: A bullet with a spear shape.

Sear: The part that holds the hammer in the cocked position.

Semi-Wadcutter: A type of bullet commonly referred to in an abbreviated form as SWC.

Shot: The discharge of a firearm. The act of shooting.

Sidearm: A weapon, pistol or revolver, carried at the side or in a belt.

Sight: Any of several devices used for guiding the eye to align it as nearly as possible with the trajectory of a firearm projectile.

Slide: The portion of a semi-automatic pistol that moves to chamber and eject the ammunition.

Small Arms: Firearms intended to be carried and operated by one person.

Single-Action Automatic: A pistol designed to be carried with the hammer fully cocked, the safety in the "on" position, and a round in the chamber.

Single-Action Revolver: Designed to fire only by manually thumb cocking the hammer which rotates the cylinder for each shot.

Stock: The wood or plastic portion of a firearm intended to be held by the hands to support the weapon.

Strong-Hand: The master hand used for firing the handgun.

Target: What you wish the bullet to strike

Thumb Safety (Safety Latch): A device which, when set, prevents the accidental firing of a gun.

Transfer Bar: A safety device incorporated in some modern revolvers.

Trigger: The finger piece of a handgun which, when pulled by a finger, releases the hammer.

Trigger Cocking: A system by which the double-action revolver cocks the hammer by pulling the trigger.

Trigger Guard: A usually curved piece of metal, attached to the frame, which surrounds the trigger.

Weak-Hand: The hand used for support of the master-hand.

Wadcutter: A type of bullet commonly referred to in an abbreviated form as WC. It has a cylindrical shape with flat ends, mainly used for match shooting with light powder charges.